How Safe is Your Home?

To Sylvia Tidy-Harris for her initial
gentle urging, changing to hard shove
which got us moving on the book.
Without her efforts and determination
this page would be blank.
MF & BT

How Safe is Your Home?

Expert advice that will reduce the risk of you being burgled

TV Burglar
Michael Fraser
and celebrated cartoonist
Bill Tidy MBE

SPRING HILL

Published by Spring Hill
Spring Hill is an imprint of How To Books
Spring Hill House, Spring Hill Road
Begbroke, Oxford OX5 1RX
Tel: (01865) 375974. Fax: (01865) 379162
info@howtobooks.co.uk
www.howtobooks.co.uk

British Library Cataloguing in Publication Data
A CIP record for this book is available from the British Library.

ISBN 13: 978 1 905862 01 6
ISBN 10: 1 905862 01 6

Cover design by Mousemat Design Ltd
Cartoons by Bill Tidy
Produced by Deer Park Productions, Tavistock
Typeset by Pantek Arts Ltd, Maidstone, Kent
Printed and bound by Bell & Bain Ltd, Glasgow

NOTE: The material contained in this book is set out in good faith
for general guidance and no liability can be accepted
for loss or expense incurred as a result of relying in particular
circumstances on statements made in the book. The laws and
regulations are complex and liable to change, and readers should
check the current position with the relevant authorities before making
personal arrangements.

Contents

About the authors

Michael Fraser

Presenter of the hugely successful BBC TV's 'To Catch a Thief' and 'Beat the Burglar' plus principal mentor of C4's 'Going Straight', Michael Fraser came within a whisker of receiving a custodial sentence as a youngster and he has not forgotten how he could so very well have gone on to become a hardened criminal had he not been given a chance to 'go straight'. Michael's childhood was not a happy one and he spent much of it in and out of care. He was expelled from more than one school, eventually leaving with no qualifications to mention. He drifted into petty crime in his early adulthood and generally seemed to be heading down a steep and slippery slope. Looking back to his youth, Michael recalls the turning point in his life. The owner of a small aluminium company was prepared to 'take a risk' and employ him as a junior. Due to his sheer fright at the looming prospect of a jail sentence Michael threw himself into his work. It was this humble start sweeping the factory floor that enabled Michael to become what he is today. He has not forgotten this, indeed it has become his personal mission to see that others can be given similar opportunities.

By working closely with the Apex Trust (he is a trustee), Michael succeeds in helping people who would otherwise struggle to get a start in life. The Apex Trust aims to help people with criminal records obtain jobs or self-employment. They achieve this aim by providing them with the skills they need in the labour market, by working to break down the barriers to their employment and increasing employment opportunities in communities with high levels of crime. Michael is able to help the Trust in many ways. He has taken on a number of employees through Apex and they have settled into their new jobs extremely well. Michael helps with raising the public profile of the Trust, having spoken at numerous meetings and appeared on several television programmes. He has become 'well known' through his three TV series, all of which received rave reviews.

Audiences readily take to him, recognising his strength of character and determination. He is fully committed to giving advice on how to avoid being the victim of crime and this was his prime motivation in writing this book. Michael is also an expert in talking business people and 'decision makers' into re-appraising their own attitudes to what makes a criminal and what can be done to turn them into useful members of society. (Sadly, the majority of kids brought up in care, end up with a criminal record and most never get out of the vicious circle of crime/institutions.) Michael has a ready wit, so any talk he gives on his life and work will make the audience both laugh and cry – but hopefully also change their attitudes and perceptions.

Bill Tidy

Bill Tidy was born in Tranmere, Cheshire on 9 October, 1933 the same year that Brits began using the American phrase 'Step on the gas!' and 'No flies on me!' from Australia. Must have some bearing on a busy life! He moved to Liverpool aged 7 for the May blitz, survived, left school at fourteen, worked in a shipping office and then joined the Royal Engineers for three years serving in Germany, Japan and Korea. He sold his first cartoon in Japan and on leaving the army joined the Pagan Smith Advertising agency in Liverpool where he learned to cram two hundred words and a drawing of a greenhouse into a one inch square space. Art School beckoned but he was asked to leave on day one because the teacher felt he had absolutely no future in art. He decided to emigrate to Canada but decided at the last minute not to go. Instead he decided to take a trip by air to London for the newly formed Cartoonists Club first meeting and sat next to Rosa, a sparkling Italian girl. They married in 1960 and had three children, Sylvia, Nick and Robert. Tragically Nick passed away in Malibu, California in 2004.

Bill's portfolio bulges with famous cartoon strips, The Cloggies, The Fosdyke Saga and several others appearing in a range of scientific, medical and archaeological publications as well as the real ale newspaper 'What's Brewing'. Bill's work has appeared in *Punch*, *Private Eye* and every national newspaper and he has presented and featured on television and radio in programmes as diverse as 'Countdown','Watercolour Challenge' and 'Tidy Up Naples!' He still derives as much pleasure out of life today, whether it is drawing as fast as he speaks on TV or narrating his 120 foot long scroll to a corporate audience on any subject, profession or calling that you name, as he did when he was a whistling office boy a long time ago.

Bill is still regularly commissioned to draw cartoons and is incredibly active on the after dinner circuit. He is delighted to be part of such a definitive and ground breaking book on home security and has great admiration for Michael whom he believes has offered optimum information which should truly change the way readers protect their homes from burglars.

Introduction by Michael Fraser

When I was a child most people didn't give me a second thought. My mother and father, my teachers, social workers and care assistants all abandoned me in one way or another and, but for a one-off chance conversation with my probation officer, I would have ended up the way of most others in my situation – in a home or prison. Of that I am 100 per cent sure!

My English mother and Jamaican father had a terribly violent relationship which was carried out mainly in front of us kids. All four of us, one brother and two sisters, were placed in care and immediately separated, which was the well meaning but incredibly cruel 'done thing' in the early 1960s.

They claimed that there was no one out there who would foster me because I was a bully and a very naughty boy. They were right and with no one to guide me and always seeking attention, even if it meant I had to do something awful to achieve this aim, I went off the tracks. I began stealing at the age of nine, was expelled from three schools before the age of 12 and was the perfect villain in the making.

What I needed was simple but unobtainable: parents, ones who loved me. Instead I was the only kid left in the home at weekends. The few times I became fond of someone I always seemed to be moved on to another home. Left on my own, I suppose because of my wildness, I observed and learned along my journey through the juvenile courts. I taught myself to read and write at the age of 14. Curiously I also learned to read people's body language, which has come in very handy particularly in business and my TV work, but that's another story.

At 16 I was caught with a stolen ring and was told that with my juvenile record I would end up in prison if I committed one more offence.

I simply stopped there and then! I had seen the damage prison did to people, youths who went in as naughty boys and came out ardent criminals and I'd had enough of institutions. I saw a job advertised and went for an interview, even though I knew I had little hope with my record and the fact that I was still on probation. The interview didn't go too well, but I was determined. I wanted the job so badly that I plagued the gaffer non-stop, and in the end he gave me the job just to shut me up!

I was put in charge of a milling machine and found that I could get on with the other workers and, better still, I was faster than anyone else at making door frames. The daily average was about 40 per person, but I wanted to knock up my earnings and was soon producing 100 plus a day! I was earning good money and decided to set up the first of my businesses which are still thriving today.

For years, thanks to my TV series Beat the Burglar, many people have asked me to produce the definitive book of anti-burglary tips. This had always been in my mind, but just like everybody else, I was so busy with work and family that I never would find the time. That is until my agent Sylvia got me in a vice-like grip and made me promise to pull together everything I knew about home security and said she would find a publisher.

True to her word she did and now I have the chance to really engage the reader with lots of cost-effective tips and eye-opening revelations which will tell you just how security conscious you are or are not! To help me get the message across I've teamed up with Britain's best loved cartoonist, Bill Tidy MBE, and together we'll make sure that the advice in the following pages is digestible but stays in the system.

The idea behind this book is not to frighten you into turning your home into a fortress! I won't be suggesting jagged pieces of glass embedded in your walls and barbed wire atop your fences, but I will ram home to you the fact that for very little cost you can avoid becoming a victim of burglary. I will ask 'how safe is your home?' and offer the guidance to help you make your home safe instead of a target.

Burglars come in different categories, but are opportunist – they see an opportunity and seize it! This means they are looking for a weak target and you the home dweller can, by doing just a little such as closing your gate and adding a padlock to a shed door, demonstrate to the opportunist that you are security conscious. If your security awareness is highly visible then the opportunist will head somewhere where it isn't.

I will provide you with an insight into how to recognise your property's weaknesses, raise your awareness of what needs to be done and tell you how to do it.

Learning from experience

Thirty years ago I was a burglar and since my involvement on the BBC's To Catch a Thief and Beat the Burglar I have become very aware of how little has changed in the way people regard their home security. Indeed I believe we are worse now than we were back in the 70s! People today are so careless about their belongings and property that it sometimes defies belief. This is a crazy attitude when you consider how incredibly devastating it is to be burgled, the horrendous affect it has on individuals, the heartache it causes and how much it costs when the insurance company hikes up your policy costs after a claim.

I can't get over the fact that many people are actually convinced that the more security they put in place, the more chance they have of being burgled! Why think that? Surely deterring someone from entering your home has to be a good thing. Another fact that staggers me is that people close their curtains when they go away; they might as well stick a sign on saying we've gone on holiday and the house is empty.

A friend of mine was so scared by his experience of a burglary that he and his family left the country. They only went away for a week's holiday and returned to find their house had been stripped. Everything had been taken including fixtures, fittings (even his underwear and the loo brush). Bizarre, horrible and shocking. Just imagine how you would feel if it happened to you.

I am deeply ashamed of what I did in my teens. Just out of care, my life was in a downward spiral, I had no one to guide me and I was in with the wrong crowd. But I thank my social worker Elaine Randall, who scared the living daylights out of me by telling me I had one more mistake to make before ending up in prison, there was a sudden and dramatic change of direction. I am eternally grateful to her as she really did get through to me and when I applied for my first job making door frames her words were ringing in my ears. Unemployed and aimless I would have ended up in prison.

Instead I put my life together and in a surprisingly short time became a successful businessman and was a millionaire at 21. It was hard work, but when I look back I can't believe how very lucky I was and still am. And the people I hung around with at that time? Most are either dead, on drugs, or serving long prison sentences.

Tackling crime

I've learned so much since my teens and feel very strongly that victims of burglary should be able to meet the burglar if they so wish. I believe that not only does it give the victims an opportunity to tell the burglar just how they feel, but helps them to find some form of closure on the whole horrible ordeal. It also provides the police officers and social workers with the opportunity to gauge the offender's reaction when confronted with an angry, tearful and shattered victim. I only wish I could have apologised to the people who were affected by my actions all those years ago.

As I gathered the material for this book I realised that in order to highlight the inadequate defences that most of you have in place in your homes, I will undoubtedly be repeating myself at times. Sorry, but I'm just trying to hammer the message home so please stay with it!

The TV series

With regard to the TV series I've made, in particular Beat the Burglar, one of the questions everyone likes to ask me is why the people taking part always look so surprised at how easily I break into their homes. It's a question I used to ask myself too, because the participants on each show applied to take part, signed up to be burgled and therefore knew I was coming! They also knew anything damaged or broken would be repaired or replaced, but still most were convinced that they could Beat the Burglar.

Needless to say not one of them did. Instead they sat in the outside broadcast van and watched the burglary take place in real time! They were often speechless, utterly stunned, very distressed and sometimes physiologically shaken! Some even lost touch with the fact that it was a TV programme and became abusive.

When it came to the point where they met the burglar afterwards I would enter with my head slightly bowed and my hands behind my back. Amazingly one furious householder threw me against a wall even though he knew it wasn't for real! Another participant was convinced that I would not get past her dog, and crumpled when she saw me on camera feeding the dog some scraps and taking it out to the car on a lead with the rest of the loot. In another programme I was actually helped by the neighbours, unaware of the hidden camera, to carry the 'stolen items' to the car.

In conclusion

I am still extremely conscious of what I did 30 years ago and am fully aware of the horrendous impact my handiwork must have had on the victims.

Luckily I was given a chance and am now helping ex-offenders through the APEX charitable trust. This helps people with criminal records obtain appropriate jobs or self-employment, by providing them with the skills they need in the labour market and by working with employers to break down the barriers to their employment. I also employ a number of ex-offenders in my businesses. Sadly some are beyond hope and help, but many like me all those years ago do change for the better and become decent, law abiding citizens.

I couldn't have done this without Bill Tidy's huge input. His humour and ability to transform my words and experiences into print have blown me away.

This is an easily read, conversational book with invaluable tips. Although reading victims' experiences of being burgled will be unpleasant, between us we can make sure that it will never happen to you!

chapter 1
Personal Experience of Burglary

'It all happened in such a short space of time'. Burglary victims always say the same thing. They moved from one room or floor to the next, just for a couple of minutes, and the intruder had been and gone. A third of all break-ins occur during daylight and we should give thanks that Coronation Street isn't shown on daytime TV or the incidence would be much higher.

The majority of offences take place towards the end of the evening or in the small hours, when people's vigilance is either distracted or non-existent. The householder suddenly spots that something is out of kilter in the normal heartbeat of the home: a curtain blowing at an open window, a drawer left open, small images which at first cause puzzlement and then become stomach churning disquiet.

Burglary of an occupied house

These were the reactions of a couple, Betty and Frank, living in Walsall in 1977, when they discovered that they had been visited. Like the American tourist who could not understand why Windsor Castle had been constructed so near to noisy old Heathrow, they were victims of those thoughtless fools in the 1920s who built houses so close to the M6. If you live near anything which begins with a big 'M' and it's not a McDonalds your thief is on his way home by the time the law shows up! This is a huge fact to be aware of that the dangers of the motorway don't necessarily begin when you fall asleep at the wheel.

Here's Mrs Betty P telling us what happened next. No drama, no evidence, no trace.

'Frank, retired and busier than ever, loved sport and liked to relax with the TV control watching the progress of any kind of ball that could be carried, kicked, struck or poked. He sat with our dog Minty downstairs in the lounge while I turned down the bed upstairs. When I'd finished it was time to make our usual night-time drink so I switched off the bedroom and the landing lights and went down to the kitchen. I gave Frank his drink and took mine back upstairs. When I switched on the landing light I noticed that the bedroom door was shut, which was odd because I'd left it open. When I went inside I saw my jewellery box standing open on the dressing table with some of its less valuable contents scattered around it. I called out to Frank who was passed on the stairs by Minty who was barking furiously. Most of my jewellery had gone. I cried and became very emotional when I realised that I might have come face to face with the burglar when he was in the bedroom. I felt even worse when I imagined what would have happened if Frank had confronted him.

Modus operandi

'It is a horrible thought that someone has been busily sorting through your possessions, discarding some items as worthless and bagging others to sell. The police arrived and recognised the burglar's modus operandi. They thought they actually knew him, but had to concede that because of the proximity of the motorway there was no hope of catching him. He'd probably been watching and waiting for the upper floor to go dark and a subsequent search showed that he'd broken through the en suite bathroom window.

'Minty was too old and deaf to notice anything less than the obvious, but you can't throw out an old friend because he's a pensioner so he was let off with a caution.'

Frank and Betty recovered from the intrusion but she made a vow…

'To always make sure that the upper floor lights are left on and that the alarm system is activated, either when we retire for the night or when we go out. We won't be victims a second time!'

There's a lesson learned, but as is often the case, a little late in the day and in a flood of tears. Your insurance can replace the material objects, but what about the other private, sentimental things of no value to anyone but yourself that were hoovered up in 'the short space of time' we started out with? Frank and Betty were an elderly couple, but burglars don't discriminate over age and the younger amongst us are as vulnerable as OAPs.

Burglary of an unoccupied house

Thieves are also pretty easy-going about working when we are celebrating, as Miche Broad, wife of ex-England cricketer Chris Broad, learned one New Year.

'It was the 30th of December and I had just returned from a wonderful holiday in South Africa. It would have been even better if Chris had been with me, but at the last minute he had been contracted by the ICC to referee a test series in New Zealand. I had arrived home in Nottingham, collected the dog from the kennels, unpacked and then repacked to spend New Year with friends in the south. I told my neighbour where I was going, how long I'd be away and left a contact number. It's quite a hike from Nottingham to East Sussex, so at 11am the dog and I set off on the four-hour trip. We arrived on time, the celebrations were tremendous fun and after a very long day I crashed into bed.

'New Years Day dawned and we were all breakfasting on strong coffee when the phone rang. I was surprised when our host said that the call was for me. It was my next door neighbour, sounding very upset as she told me that she had gone into the house to make sure all was well and found a scene of absolute chaos. Burglars had broken in and could I return home as soon as possible.

'It is a horrible feeling climbing into you car in the knowledge that at the end of a long drive you will enter your home and find it barely recognisable. This was an understatement, because it was as if a tornado had swept through with drawers up-ended and their contents thrown around, every door on every cupboard and wardrobe wrenched open, and piles of books and articles of clothing heaped on the floor. The office had been turned upside down in a snowstorm of paper, and the little strong box in which we kept our private documents broken and thrown down the stairs.

'It was such a sickening sensation to see so many of our most treasured possessions casually and brutally flung anywhere in the wild rush to find something more valuable. It was a while before I could get round to making an inventory of all that was missing, smashed or ruined and every room had a casualty: a necklace given to me by my mother, of no value to anyone but myself, cricket memorabilia, share certificates, pictures, photographs, all damaged or stolen.

'My neighbours and the police were very kind, but what could they do? We had no burglar alarm system. Why should we if we lived in, as we naively believed, a safe area peopled by decent folk?

'I had an even greater shock when I was told by the police that whoever had set up the break-in had probably watched me leave the house, with bags and dog, two days before.

'Chris was in New Zealand so I was on my own, and when I sat down after the first attempts to clean up the mess, anger and resentment flooded over me. How dare these evil, rat people sneak into our home and steal or destroy what had taken us years of hard work and saving to accumulate. Then surprisingly I thought OK, no one was hurt, they didn't foul our bed or pee in the cutlery drawer so it can all be put right.

'Well yes, except that when you are sitting alone with another five weeks to wait before Chris can come home, every creak and groan of the house and each tiny sound makes you wonder if they are back to steal the car and anything else they'd over-looked. My spare set of car keys had been taken, and I was still waiting for locks to be changed and bars fitted to the windows where the burglars had broken in at the side of the house.

'It does take a while to get back on an even keel and the burglary leaves a deep scar. Still today, several years later, when I return home and open the front door it is a huge relief to find the house 'whole' and not violated by nasty specimens who are too lazy and wicked to earn an honest living of their own.'

Reactions to assaults on property

Two slightly different reactions to similar assaults on property and possessions which demonstrate how our attitudes towards crime have changed over the years. Betty, in the Walsall account, was more apprehensive about what Frank, 67 but no pushover, would do to the intruder than anything else. To her age group a burglar has no rights and if he doesn't clear off smartly he gets what is coming to him, whereas Miche's anger turned to relief when she thought 'ok, no one was hurt in the burglary'. By this she meant the innocent victim, not the thief!

Completely different approaches to changing times, but with the constant that security was either slack or non-existent.

In Walsall the ground floor was lit while the upstairs lights were being turned off in a sequence that told a watcher exactly in which direction the victim was going!

Over in Nottingham, they relied on a safe neighbourhood and decent people rather than an alarm and they weren't let down. No neighbour robbed them and it was a nice safe neighbourhood, which is why it was in the 'very interesting' section of the thief's street guide. Not many burglars would expect to profit from working in droves on the Cutthroat estate, so they look for somewhere green and pleasant.

Learning the lessons

I think two victims' stories are enough to convey the shock, fear, anxiety and anger aroused by a burglar, so from now on we are going to minimise the chances of it happening to you. If you saw my Beat the Burglar series on TV, I'm sure the violence must have angered you. The violence was not against people, but property: door panels savagely kicked in, mattresses and furniture thrown aside like worthless rubbish as a home becomes a wreck.

I can stop this happening to you if you learn from the advice on defence in these pages and it's not all 'buy this' or 'lay a mine-field there'! Most of what I say is that rare commodity, commonsense, and it won't be long before you think like I do on security matters. There's no learning by rote and you won't be asked to recite the last 20 pages from memory.

In fact my comments and the drawings accompanying them, even if they may seem sarcastic, flippant or even funny when dealing with a serious subject like security, work on the 'Old Bill' principle used by soldiers on the front line: 'however bad things are, a joke always goes down well in the trenches'. Good teachers made us laugh as we learned at school, so remember whichever way we learn defence, our one aim is to deter the burglar and push him off to try a house whose occupier doesn't care as much as we do. Let's go!

Before we start, here's a sample of security from Ventham and Brennan's Cops 'n' Robbers anthology. A male law student phoned the police to report the theft of a mountain bike. 'You'll be able to recognise it because I put my postcode on a piece of paper inside the tyres.'

chapter 2
There's Nothing Worth Stealing in My Home!

W e all have the Big House mentality. There is our home with its cracked tiles in the bathroom and the door which needs painting. Then there is their house, the huge place with the electric gates and slavering rottweilers chasing James Bond through the grounds. It's on the same level as the Big Heist in Vegas, where the team plan meticulously to lift 50 million dollars, or those big art and bullion jobs that shock the world.

Everyday crime

This kind of glamorous criminality takes place at a safe distance from Grilby Close. It has been made to look enormously entertaining with its fabulous locations, gorgeous stars and special effects, but unfortunately these dramas omit one depressing detail.

The movies and television influence our thinking so greatly that while we are continually reminded by the media of burglary and theft, we still allow ourselves to forget that just as there are big jobs masterminded by evil geniuses there are many, many tiny jobs performed just as well by perfectly ordinary professional and amateur thieves and cheats. These are mainly men, but while I can't ever recall seeing a woman up a drainpipe, I suppose no occupation is sacred these days! Before you know it Tracey will be at the Court of Human Rights claiming that PC Williams looked up her trouser leg as he cautioned her while she was 15 feet in the air.

A living oxymoron

These criminals' quiet, unheralded work is usually practised with skill and expertise, but some find temporary fame in front of the beak. Many end up inside, but one apprehended Nottingham thief was a living oxymoron! This character was finally nailed and, as is usual, asked for other jobs that he'd done to be taken into consideration. This is done so that his glaring honesty will dazzle the judge and also save him from being done another 95 times. Consequently the police went through the score checking each burglary.

Call number ten found the police officer listening to the voice at the other end calling to his wife 'Glenda, have we been burgled?' A voice in the background was heard and the man replied to the officer that 'no, we haven't been burgled, thank you.' That was when the old panto routine began. 'Oh yes you have' said the officer and this was followed by a scream! The thief had been so efficient that they were not aware that they had been turned over. Looking back with a stroking of chins they thought 'Good God, all of those things that we thought we'd mislaid or lost, hadn't been lost or mislaid!' They were taken by a sneaking thief who had padded around their home picking and choosing from their possessions.

Insurance

On the other hand items are often taken by the fairies so, to safeguard your belongings, it won't do any harm when you update the insurance to have a good look around and check that everything is still there. On a happier note, you might find something that you really did lose years ago.

Photographic records

Whether you're in or out of luck, the best way to sort out what you have and haven't got is to take photos of every room. Forget the holiday snaps, and make a record of what each room looks like and what is in it. Take a few shots from different angles, so that if you don't follow what I am trying to get across about home security and you do have a visitor you can prove to the insurance company that your claim is an honest one.

It's a complete anomaly that when a burglary is committed it's the victim of the crime who is left with the burden of proof. Crazy, but that's how it works, and it will work even better if you mark stealable items indelibly and unobtrusively with your postcode or something personal like what is written on grandma's tattoo.

Taking precautions

Not every burglar is as good as the oxymoron moron and not every housebreaker is sufficiently psychotic that he will stub out his fag-end on your nice new white carpet. When there is damage that looks like mindless vandalism, in most cases he's turned over the plant pots, and tipped vases and boxes over in a search for keys taped to the undersides. That's what you get for trying to be clever!

Please don't dream up ingenious and crafty hiding places for jewellery and keys, because these are all on the intruder's checklist and the first place he'll look will be where you put them. He won't even have to go through his mental itinerary for the first few locations because they are automatic responses in a burglar's nervous system. Without thinking he'll lift the lid on the cistern in the toilet, where some bright spark who saw the big restaurant massacre in The Godfather has cunningly placed the key to the safe. After that or before – it depends on his mood – he'll bend down and run his hands along the hem of the curtains feeling for bulky objects that often turn out to be, you've guessed! Jewellery!

Assaults

It's the burglar's job to know the hiding places where people are foolish enough to conceal their goodies, but by saying this I am not setting up the housebreaker as some kind of master thief. According to a recent police profile the average robber is some-where between the dimwit who ends up with his foot trapped in a grid and a man who is pretty streetwise and reasonably fit.

The possibility of him attacking you is remote and when sussed he will be gone before you know it, so don't shoot him! Our laws prohibit aggressive protection and we have to defend on the back foot, so my point is that we have to keep the thief outside in the cold where he belongs.

Where assaults do occur, these are down to very sick people. I can't offer any advice on coping with a psychopath other than telling you how I would react. I would fight for my life as you must fight for yours and remember that these aren't the Marquis of Queensbury rules! Nobody is defenceless when they have a thick skull to use as a weapon and that includes you ladies. Not many thieves enjoy having their nose broken and you've bought precious escape time.

You and the thief

The whole business of crime is unpleasant, so let's get back to housebreaking and talk about you and the thief. The burglar stands on the lower rungs of the criminal ladder and doesn't aspire to greatness. All he seeks out of life is the opportunity to steal and sell on, to mix with riff-raff of his own persuasion, and to avoid paying any kind of tax that you and I are mug enough to cough up. Naturally he will shun all forms of labour requiring regular attendance, and with his knowledge of the law and state benefits he will be more than happy to shelter under the generous wings of the social services when there is a tightening up in security.

It's almost laughable when you realise that you are trying to put him on the dole, a lifestyle in which he will indulge at your expense. Not mine! Keep me out of this because my home is Fort Knox secure. No, he's leeching off you!

We are depressingly familiar with reports of theft and burglary, and we most likely know someone who has been turned over, but you will be surprised by a curious fact. Police statistics reveal that only 42 per cent of all crime is reported to the law. I can't imagine how you know something hasn't been reported, but if you think a little more deeply it becomes clearer. Apprehended criminals admit to other offences and if their confessions don't tally with recorded crimes the omission becomes apparent. But then the big question arises: why didn't the victim report the incident to the police?

The victim's reaction

The answer is simple and down to human nature. The victim thinks the whole affair is too trivial, and the law can't or won't be bothered when they have more serious business like keeping an eye on terrorists and motorists. However the excuse that most pleases the burglar is that his target is either too embarrassed or humiliated to own up. This sometimes is the dark area where large sums of money in the house might require detailed explanation, but mostly it's because the victims feel utterly scared and stupid.

Who would want to rob us?

Until we are robbed most of us feel subconsciously that it is not going to happen to us. This is a 'decent neighbourhood with nice people' – you'll hear that description continually – so we sleep peacefully behind our absolutely minimal defences. Who would want to rob us? A thief would have to be pretty hard up to make anything out of our bits and pieces! We've got the odds and sods that everyone collects, but honestly don't have anything that would even be worth breaking on the Antiques Road Show, never mind riches to attract a thief! Would any yobbo be daft enough to risk ending up inside for a few quid and a handbag?

We wouldn't like it to happen of course and our big labrador wouldn't either. Blackie's great with the kids, but you should see him go for the window cleaner and the postman! You can't imagine any intruder hanging round too long with those teeth clamped around his ankle. No worries there. We'd be picking up bits of burglar for weeks!

Be honest! Was that you speaking? Do you really think that there is nothing or very little in your home that a burglar couldn't turn into cash? Would you have to tell your neighbours next day that a night-time visitor had been so saddened by the quality of your possessions that he had left a condolences card with a fiver inside? Would the criminal be shunned by his scornful colleagues and end up in St Fagin's Home for Fallen Burglars loved only by his faithful rat?

The intruder's haul

Don't worry! You will be spared any such shame and embarrassment because I can offer a cast iron guarantee that if you have been done while on holiday or doing the school run, your intruder has left the premises with a very decent takeaway. He'll be enormously pleased that his immediate social calendar, drinking, betting and lounging around doing absolutely damn all, is assured while yours is blighted.

The legacy

You will find it hard to forget that a stranger, possibly a dirty, unclean type of man, has stolen your bits and pieces and maybe had a drink out of one of your cups. On top of revulsion there is a very unpleasant and frightening experience to live with as well, because your privacy zone has been penetrated and believe me men find the sexual overtones just as humiliating as women do.

You've already read the comments of victims of burglary and theft. While they put on a brave show they will never forget how they felt that day or night when a silent visitor came. Someone walked through their home making expert evaluations like a night shift auctioneer, made several selections and left without making any bids.

These 'someones' are regretfully multiplying because, while the police claim that the statistics on house breaking show a reduction, the chances of a victim recovering anything smaller than a horse are practically nil and in Shergar's case definitely zero! You will not get it back. Furthermore it is government policy to keep the young offender out of prison, so he might as well come to your home as anywhere else if the worst he expects is a slap on the wrist.

The statistics

In 2002 nearly 4 per cent of all households in the UK were burgled. Can you imagine that – and I don't mean rhetorically. I want you to picture your road, street or avenue and if the house numbers range from one to 100 there's a very good chance that four of them will be broken into and items stolen. Let's analyse it even more chillingly. The percentages show that in a block of 25 houses, or only 12 facing each other, one is marked down for theft and damage. Statistics are a pain, but today's polls and information gathering on anything you care to name are amazingly accurate and give fair warning of what is most likely to happen tomorrow.

SARA

One police force uses an information gathering system called SARA.

S is for scanning

An in-depth survey picks out clusters of criminal acts of all kinds and gives us a map of the entire onslaught. Of course unlike a war game there are hundreds of enemies all working independently, so the whole mess has to be laid out in some form of readable fashion.

A is for analysis

This is a detailed correlation of all information regarding dates and times, down to the hour and location where incidents have taken place. The picture is less confusing now and continual trouble spots can be discerned. For example, one type of crime regularly happens at location X and usually around mid-morning, while approaching evening another cluster of antisocial offences appears to be a constant feature over at location B. The map is another step towards prevention and, while analysis doesn't predict down to the last second where an incident will evolve, the knowledge gathered leads to the next step.

R represents response

This is a moot point these days when the public in general finds that the response that we grew up to expect from the police is no longer automatic and rapid. The force, constipated by paperwork and sometimes inclined to go for easy collars like traffic offenders, is undermanned and every police action that the public used to accept as obvious and necessary now has to be carefully considered under the straitjacket of Human Rights.

The situation is not quite as bad as some hysterical newspaper reports, based on 'call us back next Wednesday if he continues to hit you with that iron bar' make it out to be, but these stories, although a long way from the truth, are not as far as most of us would prefer. Response is not what it should be and the average citizen feels that he or she pays for a service that leans too

The police promised rapid response if we let them have a speed camera in the lounge!

heavily on speed cameras rather than deeper involvement in the more strenuous but reassuring personal intervention in robbery, hooliganism and assault.

This is true to an extent but, to put everything in a correct perspective, ask yourself to whom you turn if you become a victim of an accident or a criminal act. Of course there are bad coppers, but the majority of policemen do their difficult and sometimes dangerous job extremely well and there are not many countries on this globe where the population would echo that sentiment.

A equals assessment

Assessment looks back at what happened over a certain period and reaches conclusions. Did we win or was it another defeat?

That is the way it is done today, but as far as I am concerned SARA and all of the other acronyms are immaterial because when it comes down to the wire, my home and its security is my responsibility. You cannot hand over the safety of all of the material things you possess to the police in the same way that you entrust your children to their teachers at school. It is your burden and nobody else will thank you for carrying it. Why should they? If nothing happens and your home isn't violated, what is there to say? 'Well done, old chap. You weren't robbed this week!' Not one soul apart from yourself will know that it was worth going to the trouble of following the precautions that I am banging on about.

Mind you, if the careless, negligent, nice people next door allow themselves to be turned over you might be allowed to blow a quiet internal trumpet as you offer commiserations and perhaps even a spot of advice!

Masterminds or dimwits?

This is a serious business and we have to look after ourselves, but there's no chance of my holding your attention without injecting a little sunlight into the doom and gloom. So throughout the book I am hoping that my natural optimism and cheeriness will shine through. The criminals themselves will help us on our way, and if the lighthearted passages and drawings in this book need reinforcing then turn your mind to crime reports you have read revealing how big a mess some evil masterminds get themselves into.

Many thieves are very good at what they do, but their professionalism is counterbalanced by the large contingent of hopeless dimwits who work very hard to end up trapped in some utterly ridiculous and embarrassing situation. Then they have the cheek to expect their intended victims or the police to haul them to safety, and sometimes it works as the rooftop nitwit who demanded cigarettes and fried chicken proved. After all he'd only tried to steal a car and then pelted people with slates before he smoked, was fed and brought safely to earth by a cherry picker.

Burglary isn't what it was!

Now back to business. You are in positive danger of being burgled, and the police are undermanned, so it is time to form the wagons into a defensive circle and start thinking. I'm the wagon master and it's my job to alert you to the dangers outside the perimeter of this book and to start you thinking realistically about protecting what you value.

I can see that you are still a little baffled about my claims regarding the hidden goodies around you because you know your home and its contents. They're all neatly listed in the insurance documents and – ah! Are they? Don't be so sure. In fact most of them will not even be mentioned by name or type, which is why the first exercise in this book is to send you to the kitchen and when you say 'there's nothing in here, what's he on about?', I explode and tell you exactly what I'm on about! So go to the kitchen.

Valuable objects don't come in any particular order, but they are always in the right room and a thief knows where to look for them. Kitchens, bedrooms and studies lead the way and it's in these rooms that you'll catch up on what a thief learns on his mother's lap in the pub. The first lesson is that burglary isn't what it was in his Daddy's day! It's a different game. We now have a complete change in criminal opinion on what is and what isn't worth bagging up for the car boot sale or pub car park.

What a thief looks for

The glory time of plundering chests of gold and jewels went out with Captain Morgan and striped jerseys and our thief won't look at the blender unless he's hooked on carrot juice. These things are too cheap and available to everyone already. So much of what he's looking for is in that jungle of envelopes and bits of paper jammed into that little wooden rack thing you picked up on holiday in Spain last year.

You remember! It was meant for Auntie Sheila but she fell off the twig and it sat there for a while before becoming a magnet for envelopes, bills, cards and anything else that could be forced into it. It's a colourful little souvenir with a badly painted picture of a Spaniard's idea of what a Brit thinks a Spaniard looks like. Pedro is a fat, jolly little chap, a moustachioed man straight out of the Magnificent Seven in a sombrero and wearing a toothy grin. The wooden rack is a cemetery for things you say you'll attend to when you get home from work and forget. After the burglar's visit Pedro's smile will not be quite so toothy!

What can the crook hope to find of value? Well, thieves and burglars will never be nuclear physicists, but they are not that stupid and they know that every kitchen is almost identical. We spend a great deal of time in the engine room and the intruder can see the evidence in the rack. Hmm, that's the bank statement you intended to check and file tomorrow but didn't. It tells him quite a bit about you: shared account, whether you shop upmarket or down, standing orders, your current financial position, cheque numbers and so on. Incidentally, always check your bank statements with the greatest of care. It's bad enough being robbed by a human being without a computer turning you over!

The paperchase

Oh goodie! There's a book of cheque stubs with a couple of receipts folded up inside. Receipts are always useful because they sometimes have signatures on them and Mrs Thief could even use them if she invents a dispute with the shop over something her mother, who is too ill to come out, had bought and lost. Worth a try! Better still if it's dated for the recent purchase of an item costing £100 upwards it will give the thief a clue to the object's whereabouts in the house – wardrobe, study, garage, garden, etc.

Those tatty bits of paper in the rack might be helpful so let's look through them. Most of them end up on the floor as rubbish, but there's always the off chance that one or other of the occupants of the house can't remember vital personal data and have decided to write passwords or usernames on paper scraps. They stay around for ages, but the best record of all is Mr and Mrs Smith's equivalent of the royal circular on show in all of our homes. Can you guess what gives the daily news of the family for the next 12 months? It's fixed to the kitchen door, but we'll go a little deeper into that failing in Chapter 4.

Personal information

Diaries are worth looking for. Lots of personal information all neatly laid out and who knows, there might even be details of an indiscretion or illicit affair that could be passed on in the pub to someone who deals in silence. Information is the key word these days and you should remember that criminals keep up with developments in technology as well as wall climbing and smashing door panels.

Consider how many homes have a desktop computer these days and those of us who leave our laptops lying around the house as well. So tell me why do so many of us carefully note our user-names and passwords, and pin to the wall or write them down in a little note book which is conveniently kept in a locked desk draw? You couldn't make it easier for the burglar who doesn't even have to steal your machine. All he needs to do is swich on, log in and hey presto he has access to all your files, email address book and personal data. He can save what he needs on a memory stick and if he is feeling mischievous he can simply wipe it clean leaving you in the cart.

There's a ten million page book to be written on computer fraud, but I will not be writing it just yet as I am watching our man nip around to the back of the house. If he can't find what he wants in the cyber world he knows that most people carelessly discard spoiled or used paperwork, so why not have a scientific rummage through your wheelie bin to retrieve some scraps! He hates anti-climbing paint, but doesn't mind custard, potato peelings and slimy stuff on his hands because he's already wearing gloves. It is an amazing fact that some people, honest and the other kind, make a very good living out of bin mining! Yuk to you, but all in a day's or night's work for them.

Digging for dirt

Usually these people are looking for scandal and political dirt, but if in your case the crook excavates information, personal, financial or any kind of data that will encourage him to either call you later or exploit you immediately, you will regret throwing it away. We used to pity the poor folk who lived as scavengers on the rubbish tips of Cairo and India, but see how the quality of rubbish has changed as more and more of the results of high technology can be thrown away with the dead flowers.

It's a crazy situation, but remember we are not dealing with the crushing poverty of the third world. Our objective is defending ourselves against wasters who draw benefits from the state with one hand and take our possessions with the other. They have no scruples or consideration for anyone or anything but themselves. They operate to a set of rules unlike ours, but they know our laws better than you do and are very happy to shelter under them when it is to their advantage. Very unfair, but it is up to us to defend ourselves and our glorious wheelie bins to the bitter end. More of wheelie bins later!

Defending ourselves

As already mentioned, unlike those living in other countries we are not allowed to defend ourselves aggressively so we are forced onto the defensive. It has to be looked at as a battle of wits and imagination. While the thief has the advantage of surprise, we can discourage the marauder and send him to look for an easier target. If that sounds callous and tough remember the Bible quote 'the Lord helps those who help themselves'. And it wasn't referring to burglars!

Credit cards

Credit cards are very welcome to the thief, and the neat and tidy person who keeps all 96 of his or hers in one place like a wallet or handbag is asking for grief. If you do lose or have all of your cards stolen it's a real inconvenience, so you should always keep one out on its own, in reserve. This has the added advantage of saving money by not using it, which must be the best thing to happen to you since Christmas.

Never, never write down your PIN number on a piece of paper. Memorise it, like your name and address, and if you have difficulty in remembering who you are, where you hang out and what your sock size is scratch the number on the inside of your watchstrap.

On the other hand it doesn't matter if you engrave the number on the inside of your eyelids if a loitering observer can see what you are feeding into the machine. I find the protective shield over the pad to be as much use as the Vatican synchronised swimming team, but at the moment, however flawed the system is, PIN is the best security we have. Doubtless the cunning Professor Moriarty will find a way round the system, but until then we must learn to remember, to love and live with numbers.

Securing your PIN number

Here's a guaranteed and simple method of ensuring the secrecy of your PIN. It's only a pit stop on the first lap of the security grand prix, but try it. When you are somewhere like a shop or garage there is usually a small queue of assorted fellow customers and, possibly, a villain close enough to breathe down your neck as you prepare to tap the code into the little machine on the counter.

If you sense that someone is standing just a little too closely turn your head slowly, and with a smile sweep everyone present with the classical but silent 'you looking at my bird?' expression. You'll be surprised as they all self-consciously step back a pace! It doesn't have to be a violent or aggressive movement, or centred on any one person, but it's a part of human nature that

most of us, particularly Brits, seem to respect the privacy of others and we feel embarrassed if this is pointed out to us.

The Japanese adopt a different approach. Recently in London I saw two young female tourists at a cash point. They stood back to back, one tapping in and the other staring stoically into the distance as a perfect human shield. If both participants wanted to make a withdrawal it would be interesting to watch the reverse manoeuvre. They do much the same with the guard-changing at Buckingham Palace and if you look closely you might just see the cards in their bearskins.

Security in the study

Back to the box stuffed with letters and the usual junk mail, which he'll ignore unless he needs the latest miniature deaf aid, private medicine or new credit card deal. By the way, don't think that the guard dog is forgotten. I will come back to the imagined security offered by the terrifying Blackie in another chapter, because it is now time to move on to other rooms in the house where there won't be so much paper, but some really good stuff. We will assume for demonstration purposes that the occupants are out somewhere having a wonderful time and will not be back for a while, so let's see what is on offer today.

The thief is hoping for a study, den or wherever people – mostly men – get away from the family. He's in luck on this trip, but if there isn't a study he knows that the valuables will probably be in the master bedroom. It's just that it saves time going through desk drawers and he doesn't get sidetracked by items from Janet Reger. Naturally the door isn't locked and, just as true to form, the desk or bureau is impregnable to anything but a hairpin or piece of plastic.

In the desk

Some desks come from auctions, huge mahogany brutes which help the owner to imagine that he's running the universe instead of working in the council planning department, but the vast majority were spotted on the Screw-U-Too Office Furniture Company website. It was 'our big sale must end this week' week and security came second to price.

These desks were for offices, so why should they be built to withstand a nuclear blast or bent coat hanger? Who would want to steal Miss Henderson's knitting or the Duke of Nerkleby's reserve glass eye? Quite correct, but Miss Henderson didn't take personal documents to the office and keep them in her flimsy desk – important stuff like her passport, for instance. Yet the owner of this house keeps the whole family gallery of passports in his desk and even the pathetic red EU passport, which is not a patch on the old blue hardback version that he used to steal, is worth good money in the wrong hands. Identities and identity fraud is big business so straight into the bag they go.

Your driving licence

Today's driving licence is a nuisance, with the plastic euro thing and its photo of Popeye (well, that's what mine looks like) and then the full licence which is a sheet big enough to cover the wicket at Lords. Nevertheless burglars do not allow personal likes and dislikes to influence choice and there are a few people knocking about who would feel happier driving around with your licence than theirs, if they ever had one! That's you faced with ringing Swansea for the rest of your life and filling in forms that keep sending you back to Part 111 Section 197 while the thief has trousered another few quid.

Your mobile phone

The thief can actually see the mobile phone that you will be looking for to make your call to the police, only to find that it isn't there! That becomes part of the catch as well and, while it won't last long, he'll get a few calls out of it on your account. Which reminds him, he might pull the phone wires out of the wall for the hell of it.

Other desk gems

There's a lot of rubbish in the desk, but he can still sift a few gems. There are some insurance forms, mortgage details, repayments on the car, a legal wrangle with a neighbour, etc – all personal information with names, facts and figures which would enable an impostor to slip into and really interrupt the flow of your private and business life. Identity theft is a huge worldwide criminal activity. Imagine how you would feel, having been trapped in a ten-mile queue on the M25 on the 9th October, when your next credit card statement informs you that on that date you were spending £5,000 on jewellery in Hong Kong!

Business security

If you are running a business from home and are not watertight secure you really deserve to be turned over. You've worked very hard to get your little show on the road and if either of your two office staff stole kit you would be enraged, so why on earth leave your home open? Ask yourself 'am I the only one who can use a laptop or read a company report?' The chances are that the thief is reasonably computer literate, or has a mate who is, and when he sees your laptop he'll have the choice of using it for information or taking it home for the kids.

The computer itself is worth peanuts, but even if you save everything you were for a short time sharing confidential information with a criminal, so keep it secure. He knows your cash flow, borrowings, contracts and every other minute detail of the small business that you have sweated blood to build. If you have cut corners with the VAT and the Inland Revenue, oh dear...

The steal or return principle

This leads us into another aspect of theft, one that I think is even more contemptible than going through a home and taking objects of intrinsic value. This is the thief who operates on the steal or return principle.

Your insurers, however reluctant you imagine them to be, will eventually pay out what is an agreed fair estimate of the value of the articles missing as a result of the robbery. Good, but what of other items which do not fit into the normal scale of evaluation? I'll get to them in a moment when we look around the bedroom, because it is here that we are at our most unimaginative. 'Hold on!' I hear you say, 'speak for yourself because Esmeralda and I often jump off the wardrobe!' Fair enough, but let's get back to the burglar.

The first thing he will look at is the dressing table and its contents. He is almost certain that madam's little box of jewellery will be there. It's nearly always the dressing table because if you are unable to see yourself in the mirror how can you tell if the earrings make you look like Olive Oyl? The alternative of placing mirrors everywhere is an excellent idea, but a little tricky and will lead to a spate of stories in the neighbourhood. If the crown jewels aren't in the dressing table, chances are that they'll be hidden in the underwear drawer or lurking beneath the bed.

Wherever the damn thing is, when he finds it he's not really expecting to stumble on the lost treasure of the Incas in a five ton safe. He doesn't rob in those circles, but is fairly confident that there will be something in that little box that is untraceable and worth 50 quid in the pub on the estate.

Stealing memories

On the other hand he might just be in luck and find something really special tangled up in the strings of imitation pearls, tacky high street bracelets and fake gold watches – an object that is relatively worthless, even ugly, but beyond price. It might be a handed down brooch, in the family since Auntie Florence was hanged for rustling, or a ring or something Uncle Fred brought back from Japan where he was a prisoner of war. Whatever it is it represents an absolutely priceless memory to the family and they would be utterly devastated if it was stolen. What's more, and here's the good news, they'd pay anything to get it back!

This is where steal and return comes into the equation. Greedy thugs have no feelings or respect for the memories of their victims and if you want them back, it'll cost you. I hope that by now I have convinced you that you were way off beam when you said that there was nothing in your home worth stealing – and we haven't mentioned your wedding album yet! Can you imagine how you would feel if you were recovering from being burgled with no hope of any of the precious stolen articles being restored and the telephone rang. 'Mrs Higgins, about those missing wedding pictures of yours. Very nice. Do you want them back for 100 quid or should I burn them?'

It's been done many times. If insurance companies pay out for the return of art treasures, why shouldn't the mendacious, evil minded little creep who took the photographs, jewels or mementos of no great value to anyone but you and yours, ask you to do the same? Marriage licences, letters, souvenirs, medals, photographs, decorations, diplomas, certificates, locks of hair – you wouldn't believe it, all are fair game to a thief because he knows that they have tremendous heartbreak value and you will pay to get them back.

More collectables

The bag is becoming quite full and if he ends up with more items than expected he can always use a pillow case, or the zipped covers on the couch cushions downstairs, which you've just paid £300 to be recovered! Just by going through the drawers in various rooms he has added to a good day's/night's takings and nothing too desperately heavy yet. So what's next?

If the owner is a collector he'll have boxes, books and cases of weirdo stuff that only oddballs keep. Our thief has come across some funny collections: old fashioned cigarette cards of movie stars and footballers with centre partings, maps, butterflies, kids' comics. It can really pay off, as it did when he took those rare birds' eggs that the householder had gathered illegally. Then there was the time he called on a house and the bloke was into football programmes. Stacks of the things, hundreds in neat bundles, some new, but most in rags and tatters like Arsenal v Accrington Sidney, but a lad he knew in the pub put him on to a feller who was into football and a deal was done, no questions and lots of readies. He found a dozen stamp albums in one place, but you've got to know about stamps otherwise they are a waste of time.

Crumbs, is it that late? It's time to close the shop so he has one last look around.

Easy pickings

Pity about the grandfather clock, but it wouldn't fit under his arm and there are a few odd items worth taking. He's learned to travel light and there's a couple of hundred quid in the bag. That and the Social should see him through for the week and then he'll call this number and ask for a quote for the return of the wedding pictures. Nothing to it really! The dog will be OK in the toilet finishing his piece of steak and with a bit of luck the owners will be home to take him for walkies soon. They went out to see a movie and should be back in a couple of hours.

Two hours! Huh, he could turn the place over and redecorate the kitchen in 20 minutes! Longer if him and his mate were doing what they laughingly refer to as a house clearance, but this gaff was a solo effort and good fun.

Dos and don'ts

He's right, it was an absolute doddle! There is nothing to robbery if you, the householder, tenant, flatmate, occupier or whatever trust to luck. You are wide open, so listen to someone who knows and I will tell you how to make sure that the thief will write you off as 'very uncooperative' and move on to another target. As you go through this definitive anti-burglary encyclopaedia you'll find a list of dos and don'ts at the end of each chapter.

Every one of these little commandments is a mixture of commonsense and ingenuity. If you follow them, believe me, any decent burglar will instantly recognise a secure home and move on. The last thing he wants is to get caught, so why take chances when there are plenty of gaffs that are wide open?

- Don't leave personal documents littered around the house. Identity fraud is now endemic and your bank account or credit rating can be destroyed by an impostor.

- Do keep a file on finances and put it in a secure place like a safe that is bolted to the floor or firmly fixed in the wall. Without a financial record you are in the cart.

- Don't leave receipts about the house. Every receipt tells a story to a thief.

- Don't keep credit cards or passports all together in one place. A thief would be delighted to pick up everything he wants in one hand.

- Don't write down PIN numbers. Remember them.

- Do destroy all current or out of date personal data that has no further use. To a thief every item containing numbers, dates and codes has considerable further use. Sadly, his only use for shredded documents would be to hang them on his Christmas tree.

- Do ensure that desk drawers are secured. Lock them and keep the keys in a separate place.

- Do keep your special memories in a safe place. They are more valuable than diamonds.

- Do keep both sections of your driving licence locked away and, for added security, in separate locations.

- Don't place your jewellery in the dressing table drawer. At least make the crook work for his living!

- Don't rely on a pet to protect your home unless it is a fully grown water buffalo.

- Do keep decorations and awards under lock and key. They too are special memories.

- Do keep themed collections in a safe place. Stamps, football programmes, etc all have a rival collector out there just as fervent as you are, but not quite as honest.

- Don't leave cameras, mobile phones, diaries or expensive sunglasses on view. All of your current life is in that diary, including the cost of those expensive sunglasses!

- Do use your imagination to make life difficult for the burglar, but don't try to be too clever. He is an expert on hiding places, so forget about sewing the jewellery into the hem of the curtains and taping keys under plant pots. Concealment is out, but you can make life difficult for an intruder by putting obstacles in his path. If I say put a lock here there's nothing stopping you installing two!

I hope that you are suitably horrified at finding out that your humble abode is in actual fact an Aladdin's cave for a busy thief with no conscience. It is absolutely true, or thieves would have long ago given up stealing from semi-detached homes with four bedrooms. They're still at it, but as of now not from your home. I am going to show you how some good advice, lots of common-sense and a modest outlay will take the question mark from the title of this book and replace it with an admiring exclamation: 'by George, how safe is your home!'

chapter 3
From the Outside Looking In

Remember the old TV ads, 'the Viking Butter Man is down your street today!' and there was some poor devil dressed up as Erik the Greasy, or in other adverts he'd be a carrot or a tube of toothpaste? You couldn't miss him.

It's a shame that burglars have given up traditional costume because you probably won't spot him walking down your street today. He can be anything under 35, fairly fit and about nine or ten stone. There is no dress code as long as it merges with the night – he could be one of the millions of clones that we are all slowly turning into. He'll be proceeding in a coma on his daily round, wearing that hypnotised stare that you see on people on buses or the tube, totally disinterested and far away.

The burglar ID

Our man might look like that in his uniform of jeans, baggy denim top and maybe a bobble hat. To the casual observer he's probably a labourer on some local job. That's partly correct because he is hoping to be occupied locally and the job that he has in mind will be done on your home. He's not into gardening or putting down a new path, but is principally interested in entering your home without your consent and stealing everything that he considers that he can sell on. The rest he will dismiss as utterly worthless, although he might smash or ruin certain objects in a search to find something better.

Once inside your home, the robber's reactions depend entirely on their disposition, so the obvious response is to deprive him of the chance of examining your home and its contents. Our man is fully aware that some people do actually go to the trouble of defending their possessions, which is why he's inspecting the locality today on a reconnaissance mission. He is a professional, for his job is to enter, steal and leave without trace. What he doesn't want is trouble.

Targeting the burglary

The robber picks his time carefully, when there's not too much happening, that empty hour when Dad's just gone to work and Mum's on the school run. There are other favourable slots which are determined by the area, its activities and the time of year. Winter offers the cover of early darkness, but the risk of some nosey Neighbourhood Watch twerp wondering why a stranger is on patrol. The light of summer means that the burglar's inspection has to be much more covert, but to compensate for this unfair advantage the victims leave open their doors and windows!

Like every profession, burglary has its ups and downs. Today our unqualified surveyor and housing inspector will walk up and down your road, street or avenue looking for two types of dwellings, one that is a pushover and another that he will avoid like the plague. Here's how he reaches a decision.

What a robber loves

He starts on his way past the houses and gives each the once over. He goes through the sequences expertly and as unobtrusively as possible because time is not on his side. He can't risk going back for a second look, not today anyway, so the inspection has to be snappy and correct.

Right, the first house has a high hedge which the occupant imagines gives him some form of security. It doesn't. What it does do in its present state is condemn dad to endless hedge trimming and offer privacy to the family and any burglar crouching there waiting for his moment. The thief isn't madly in love with hedges because they can be a damn nuisance if he has to leave in a hurry, but they do offer cover in an emergency.

That's a good start and an even better sign is the half-open garden gate. Any kind of gate is a barrier, and if it is closed it might lead to a moment's fatal delay in the thief's progress as he is forced to lift the latch instead of quietly and unobtrusively slipping through. The gate itself couldn't stop a charging butterfly, but if it is closed it shows that the occupants are aware that they want the enclosed area of their home to stay that way.

This house is inviting a caller because, believe it or not, the half-open gate is twinned with an 'I'll only be out for five minutes!' fully open garage door. He makes a mental note to the effect that if the residents have not had brain surgery by his next recce he could be on to a winner.

What a robber hates

The next building is an immediate no-no. They have a burglar alarm. Normally alarms don't bother him because he knows that 75 per cent of the population just don't have the energy to activate their systems when they leave the house. They're frightened of them going off in the middle of the night and upsetting the neighbours or the police, who stamp their feet and say 'if this alarm goes off again we are not going to come! So there!' Other people have left the alarm unused for so long that they have forgotten the code. There are others, slightly more security aware, who do not wish to forget the code so they write it down by the box. More of that in a later chapter, which should be entitled 'dingbats' but isn't.

Another factor to deter the information gatherer is that the alarm box on the side of the house is bright and clean. This shouts out to him that the alarm is continually used and that the residents have had it serviced quite recently, because the engineer who does the maintenance always ends the work with a flourish of his duster to give it that nice, spanking new look. The first rule of burglary, apart from lying about your name, is always to ignore any property which looks difficult and go on to an easier gaff because there's bound to be one and, glory, here it is!

The perfect target

This place needs a lick of paint. It's not greatly rundown and there's a decent car parked in the drive, but the garage doors and some of the windows look quite rotten and he can't spot any locks on them. The owner, who obviously doesn't like painting or paying someone to do it for him, has got round most of the front door problem by putting a panel in. This is excellent news for there are not many things that burglars find more attractive than a glass panelled door. Better in the back door than the front, but anything that weakens a point of entry is a gift.

He hasn't been wasting his time here because he's just picked up on a rough symbol chalked on the side wall of the building. It tells him that old people live here and has been put there by a previous inspector who either found something better to do or is being detained at Her Majesty's Pleasure.

Thieves have a variety of signs to share with fellow lowlife indicating pensioners, mad dog, stay clear. Although not a great deal of use is made of this technique, if you notice odd chalk signs on any walls rub them out. We want no advertisements thank you, unless it's the skull and crossbones. There might not be rich pickings in that house, but it's unprotected, and if the burglar is sussed he'll disable their zimmer frames and clear off. Let's glance at next door.

Avoiding Colditz

No thanks, this is like Colditz! The outside freshly painted, expensive drapes half-closed over lace curtains stopping any shop window examination of the contents of the front rooms and nothing to see in the upstairs windows. The big garage door has a defender post mounted in front of it and the wheelie bin looks immovable. They've secured it and the bin only goes for walkies when the bin men come. How can anyone get in through a window if they haven't got a bin to stand on?

And do you know what he's done with the hedge? The miserable householder has put up a trellis fence in front of it so that he's still got the privacy of the hedge, but now the thief has to negotiate something that will collapse under him with a crash! What's more the sharp, splintered edges of the trelliswork will rip his clothes and skin and if blood is drawn they can do him from DNA samples.

The double glazing isn't very encouraging either. It looks new and secure and at this gloomy stage he'll put money on the certainty that they'll have three-hinge doors without lift-out pins. It's a nightmare. He can't see a single lock that isn't well above kicking range and would guarantee a hernia if a foolhardy attempt was made. There's no letter box either - nowhere to insert a wire coat hanger for a bit of key fishing, just a mailbox standing in full view of the world and looking like it was made during the crusades. This house is making him feel nauseous and the last blow as he walks away are the Neighbourhood Watch stickers he can see on the windows and probably every blade of grass in the garden.

He hates Neighbourhood Watch! Miserable little curtain twitchers with nothing else to do in their pathetic, empty lives but spy on thieves and warn everyone in the surrounding area that there's danger in the air. He's the one who's supposed to be furtive, watchful and sly and now there are retired chief clerks and post mistresses keeping tabs on him. But he isn't going to get anywhere worrying about the places he can't get into when he should be looking for push-overs.

A promising gaff

He'll stay on this side of the road because anyone swanning from one side to the other is just asking for the twitchers to reach for the phone. Patience and sharp observation will see him through and it does. Here's a promising gaff and what a pretty sight. A big, fat, contented pussy cat is staring at him from a ground floor front window.

He loves animals because Catz meanz Flapz and he'll bet that the back door will have an entrance for Tibbs about two feet directly under the keyhole. The flap is specially made to admit a burglar's hand holding a wire coat hanger with which he will fish for the key that is usually left in the lock because it's the back door and back doors don't count. Amazing! These people love their home and all it contains. It is well maintained and has a manicured lawn, but they still leave a hole in it all day and during the night! And that's not all.

To compound the felony, just to please that overfed moggie who likes to spend half of its life sitting in the window they've pulled the curtains back. They cost a fortune and the last thing they wanted was ' that b..... cat' climbing up them and getting its claws in the silk and brocade. Good thinking, but a false economy because just as there is nothing to stop the cat looking out there is also nothing to stop the scout looking into the room as he trundles by. A few bits of silver on the sideboard and some Chinese pots. Don't know about them, although he likes take-aways, but it all goes into the book along with the 'beware of the dog' sign.

Security awareness

Funny how the crime statistics are down 20 per cent because he hasn't noticed any great changes in security awareness. You always get the same people who care about security. These are the ones who've already been done or who have possessions that they know are worth nicking. Thank God most people have no idea what is valuable in their homes. The ones who do are some-times ex-crooks who have no intention of being turned over by former brethren, but whoever they are he's not remotely inter-ested in their property. He's looking for lambs not tigers!

A gaff too far

Baa! Here's one. It's the best house in the locale, but not really his kind of meat because the loot inside is a class above his job description of 'petty thief'. This can be very hurtful when the beak lets rip in a crowded courtroom, but our man knows his place and much as he'd like to roll up a Van Gogh and stick it down his trousers, he's streetwise enough to concentrate on the £200 turns.

Key pads

What pulls him to this place is the fact that while the owner is obviously security conscious, with his fancy electrically operated entrance gates, he has overlooked what every conscientious cleaning lady in the world would clock in seconds! The gates are operated either from the inside or by using an outside key pad which will open the gates when a certain three or four figure code known only to the owner, his missus and girlfriend is tapped in. All codes and ciphers are breakable of course, but the sight of someone standing in front of this bloke's house, rain or shine, tapping away at his key pad for 20 years trying to find the right sequence, would eventually attract attention.

Happily there is another way and like all solutions to problems it is simple, easy and obvious when you know what to look for. All key pads contain numbered studs which if pressed in the correct sequence will cause an electrical reaction. This can be at a bank cash point or in front of the gates which our friend is currently strolling past.

To give himself a little extra time he will drop something by the keypad stand and take a quick glance as he retrieves whatever it is. He will look at the keys and try to spot which are the dirtiest or most used. Once he knows the numbers involved in the sequence there are only 12 combinations of those digits and he's in.

The gardener doesn't think it's his job to clean keypads and the lady of the house doesn't either, so they become grubbier and easier to read each day.

Electric gates

Another act of laziness which helps our friend is when there is a problem with the gates and the two-pronged key which pins them until later is left in situ. Later is too late, but not for the sharp thief who slips in or out of the premises in those few short seconds between the car arriving or departing and the gates closing. If you are asking why a thief doesn't ignore the gates and climb over the wall, it's because he's thinking of his exit carrying half a ton of loot in the owner's four-wheel drive.

Carry on scouting

He's now nearly done so he turns and retraces his steps, but a little more quickly on the outward leg to allay the suspicions of any casual observer who might have noticed him earlier.

He's just passing a skip and some rubble. The house where the work is being done will have to change its routine to accommodate the coming and going of workmen and there will in all probability be different labourers and craftsmen there each day. This will provide an opening for an impersonation of a workman or delivery man and an in-depth examination of the premises. Confusion, dust and radios playing loudly are a great help, but our man isn't an opportunist thief... not unless the opportunity comes up and hits him in the face.

In fact he was just assessing a job like a builder would and it sometimes made him laugh when he heard people who had been turned over, blaming it on the lads who built the new garage when it was the work of a careful observer passing by. Anyway who wants recognition? Burglary is its own reward.

All in all, it's been a very good scouting exercise and he's learned a great deal about you and where you live. This location is close to a motorway exit so when he's got what he wants he can jump into the rattler and be in another town by the time you wake up. Some of the homes he will avoid like poison, but he can't wait to stand on that wheelie bin under the window at number 22 or do some key fishing at the House of the Big Cat. He can already see Blackie's tail wagging as he tucks into the lamb chop our man will throw into the toilet prior to locking the dog in. It's quieter and more humane than giving him a good kicking!

Dos and don'ts

That's a brief look at how your property is sussed out. Thieves use their imagination and there are always new weaknesses and sloppiness in attitudes to security so they change their tactics. You have to do the same. Here are just a few reminders of what From the Outside Looking In should have printed on your memory.

- Don't rely on your hedge as a barrier. A thief can hide in it and smash through if leaving in a hurry, but thorny bushes planted outside of the hedge will stop his rush.

- Do erect a trellis fence that will collapse under a climber. No thief will risk injuring himself and leaving blood that can be used as a DNA sample and lead to his conviction.

- Don't leave gates or outer doors open. They are an invitation and tell the thief that you are careless. If this gate is open then the chances are that another might also not be doing its job.

- Do have a garage defender post installed. If they steal your goods and use your car to take them away you will feel totally humiliated and the sympathy that others have for you regarding the theft will turn to laughter when the story is told in the pub.

- Don't rely on your dog or a 'beware' sign as a defence. Burglars have dogs and their dogs love fillet steak, pork sausages and lamb chops, but they never have them. The thief keeps them for your dog!

- Don't leave your door key in the lock above a cat flap or by a letter box. A wire coat hanger opened up into a long rod with a hook will not catch a 28lb salmon, but it is irresistible to a key.

- Do see that your wheelie bin, which makes an ideal climbing frame, is firmly anchored well away from windows.

- Do use a secure post box away from the house, with its contents out of sight, an aperture too small for a two year old thief to insert his hand and a lid with a lock.

- Ensure you pick cylinder and deadlocks on all front and back doors. Any other sort of lock should not be placed at kickable height. Neighbours may think you are mad standing with your leg against the door, but as you may have seen on my Beat the Burglar TV series, a thief can easily smash a door panel in and sometimes jump the lock with a kick. And we are not just talking about a boot or a subtle Beckham 40-yarder. This is a really violent, savage attack on the door and it only takes – bang – a second!

- Do use deadlocks and three-hinge door locks. The burglar alarm chapter will advise on this inert or passive system of security.

- Don't have outer doors with glass panels. He can see in and if there's a pile of mail on the floor then he's got an empty house at his mercy. In some homes with an alarm the DIY control box can actually be seen from the front door! Remember that any panel in a door is a weakness to the man with a flying boot.

- Don't arrange your curtains to suit the cat in the window. Cats are only interested in drapes if they smell of fish and yours shouldn't. Curtains are there for the benefit of those on the inside, not vice versa.

- Do hang lace curtains to prevent thieves looking into your rooms. The fashion police are dead against them and so are burglars!

- Do contact Neighbourhood Watch for stickers and up to date local crime information. Take no notice of those who talk disparagingly about nosey curtain twitchers. How would you feel if you were doing something illegal and all of the time there was a nagging worry at the back of your mind that curious eyes were following every movement? You would stop pinching the bricks from the building site across the road and go home.

- Do use double glazing as protection. The frame doesn't rot and the locking system is infinitely better than sash windows which are vulnerable, like many front door locks, to an expertly inserted piece of plastic.

- Do use anti-climbing paint on drainpipes. It's a nasty surprise to the unsuspecting thief, a really comfortable pair of best robber's gloves will be ruined and any further attempts on Everest or your upstairs lavatory window will be cancelled for the foreseeable future.

- Do change the key pad sequence from time to time and clean regularly used key pads, change when worn and remove the key.

- Do be vigilant on a gorgeous summer's day when too many windows are open, music is being played and the smell from your barbecue tells everyone for miles that you are all in the garden.

- Don't leave keys under the mat, a plant pot or on the door lintel. Please!

- Do a quick look around for suspicious characters when leaving or entering your home. Just a glance and if you see someone you know give them a smile. If you do spot a man who avoids looking back at you, that is a job well done because you've upset his plan of action and he will probably disappear rapidly.

- Don't allow the disturbance inadvertently caused by workmen to distract your vigilance. Make it clear that certain areas of the home are off limits and if they want anything they are to ask you or someone you designate.

- Don't allow an unrestricted view of the room where the family usually gather to watch TV. It looks cosy, but it tells an observer that the rest of the house is unoccupied and not wishing to disturb your enjoyment the thief will enter your home via the room furthest away from Coronation Street.

- Do leave landing lights on. They help jumbo jets but faze thieves. A burglar prefers the premises that he has targeted to be empty, but from street level all he can see is an illuminated window which can mean anything. Are they in or are they out? Think I'll give it a miss tonight.

> **Error of the week** – *Sunday Times* 14 May 2006
>
> *A robber tried to shoot the lock off a shop door, but got an unpleasant surprise when the bullet bounced off and hit him on the chest, say police in Victorville, California. The robber was knocked over by the bullet but otherwise unhurt!*

chapter 4
From the Inside Looking Out

L et's sit in our castle and think back on how we've improved through the years. We started in a tiny flat, then the kids came, and we upgraded to a bigger apartment and then into our first house. It was nothing special and we didn't like the people next door, but it was ours. After that we moved a couple of times – seven years is the average for living in the same situation – but what it represented was our quiet determination, without knowing it, to have a home that had enough in it to attract a thief!

Protecting your home

Sounds cruel, but that's how a burglar looks at it. There's an interesting parallel here between attitudes to children and our homes. You have protected your children every second of the day up to now and the perils of growing up in modern times makes you even more wary. Today's parents are constantly aware of peer pressure and outside influence, but you don't just throw the towel in and say 'if someone out there is hell bent on corrupting my son or daughter it'll happen. It doesn't matter what lengths Mum and I go to, if they want to do it they'll do it.'

No caring parents would acquiesce in the pollution and destruction of their child with a shrug. Yet every day I hear people say of the housebreaker 'if they're determined to get in, they'll get in!' This is absolute rubbish and infuriates me because, as I repeat over and over again, the burglar is looking for the soft touch, not hard work. If he sees obstacles that will impede his entry and swift getaway he will instantly lose interest and your little flag will drop off his map.

Being a cheeky, irreverent so-and-so he'll recover from this temporary disappointment and walk on to the next house, and the next and the next, until he finds one that is more welcoming. That is his problem, not yours, because if you have nudged him away from your home in the direction of someone who doesn't care enough to protect their own dwelling whose fault is that?

Your outer defences

Let's look first at our outer defensive ring. This is the hedge or wall with gates.

Gates

Gates always look much better when they are shut! We don't buy them to keep open. If you went home to your wife and said 'darling, look at this lovely gate I've bought as your birthday present!' the second thing she'd do – after chasing you out of the house with a frying pan – would be to look at the beautiful wrought iron and woodwork in the correct closed position.

Did you know that the inhabitants of some of HM's prisons make excellent garden furniture and gates? Whether they leave them open out of nostalgia I don't know, but however interesting and slightly incongruous this is, the fact is it doesn't matter who puts them together as long as they are kept closed. I am fully aware that enforcing this with children will be a nightmare, but the gate is your first line of defence and it is up to you to get the message across.

You are probably thinking 'why all the fuss about a gate that would not stop a Kamikaze bluebottle?' First it is still an obstacle and a thief would have to stop to open it. This might attract attention and anyone having the trouble that I have with unpredictable latches – rattle, rattle, push, push and they still don't open – could have the entire Neighbourhood Watch detachment on his back. From the point of view of a thief a closed gate indicates 'keep out' so he will look for one that isn't quite so hostile.

Hedges

We already know that the hedge serves two purposes: privacy for me as I dance naked in the front garden and cover for an intruder. He's not over the moon about lurking in a tangle of privets, but if spotted he'll find it easier and quicker smashing his way through it than climbing over a six-foot high wall and possibly turning an ankle on landing. Under normal standards of householder carelessness he could hide in the shadows until he picks his moment, but not tonight and definitely not in this hedge.

Fencing

The reason is that the man from the garden centre turned up on Thursday and delivered the kind of fencing that intruders dislike intensely.

You didn't want barbed wire, electric fencing, machine guns and searchlights so you asked the man to suggest something. He came up with trellis fencing. It looks nice and rustic, it's very light, easy and quick to erect and you laughed because he was obviously off his rocker. What use is a fence if it collapses with a noisy splintering crash when a burglar tries to climb over it?

Yours is now a hollow laugh as the garden centre specialist explains that spider man will be a human hedgehog when he eventually reaches the ground. More like a clown actually, with a bulky top that managed to catch on every twig in the hedge and with a badly scratched face to finish the picture. He's alive, but looking like a DNA advertisement and at two in the morning this is going to take some explaining if the Old Bill stops him on the way home.

The only feature in the burglar's favour is that as a freelance he can give the whole thing up as a bad job and go home, where he will probably get some earache from his partner as she plasters the wounds. The dream scenario would be if our hero arrives home in the small hours bleeding profusely and without his usual caution and she, mistaking him for a burglar, adds to his injuries.

It's a good feeling to know that we have started to make life difficult for the thief and it is going to get worse for him with our next simple obstruction. It doesn't cost the earth, it will never break down and the sound when you walk on it is so evocative of all the mystery movies you've ever seen. It's the Agatha Christie set-up where lots of well-spoken, nice people spend a weekend at a superb country house, murder each other after dinner and leave a footprint in the soil outside the French windows. What is it?

It is gravel! When I scrunch up to my front door I feel like His Lordship being welcomed home by the butler after another hard day's shooting and I can't think of any other sound apart from a shotgun going off that is as distressing to a burglar in the small hours! Gravel works in any length of approach to a house and if stealth is your aim it doesn't matter how athletic, delicate or sophisticated the thief is, it is a serious handicap.

It is difficult to walk on when the thief is hoping for a stealthy approach, and the small stones are not stable and very noisy to run on if he has to leave at speed. Of course if he is collared there will be tiny pieces stuck in his trainers or boots which would put his 'all night in the pub' alibi under some stress. Even in a tutu with several seasons at the Bolshoi behind him, a yobbo would have as much chance of a silent approach and departure as Pavlova would of dancing soundlessly on a packet of salt and vinegar crisps.

Gravel is an automatic defence that you can lay and forget about and if tied in with passive lighting puts you ahead of the thief. It's nice to have a protective measure that looks good, and there are quite a few types and colours to choose from. Sadly I have not yet been able to find the variety and colour which really irritates a thief, but personally I like light shades and a type that sounds like children eating breakfast food.

Lighting

Timed, light sensitive or activated illumination deters the thief. There cannot be anything more petrifying for a robber than to be suddenly bathed in a blast of brilliant light which hits him like a blow. The greatest strengths of passive or active lighting are its variability and your control on its use. It can be on constantly, activated by a beam being interrupted or by motion sensors, but like all technical aids it will only do as you command it to in return for regular inspection, maintenance and TLC.

The placement of your illuminations depends on the shape of the house and its grounds. Low or flat roofs attract housebreakers so keep them covered by activated lights or well lit by passive lighting.

Checking and inspecting

It's worth remembering that there are several species of thief and only the opportunist robber, as his name suggests, acts spontaneously. Conversely there is the patient housebreaker who does his homework today and intends to break in tomorrow or soon after. His technique is to slip in and interfere with the lighting, not dramatically, but enough to make you say to your wife 'that blasted bulb has gone again and I'll replace it at the weekend if I don't forget.'

His hope is that you will forget or even that you are too tired and can't be bothered to do your nightly inspection of the estate, even though you know that the line is breeched. He understands human nature and is aware that if you are tired after the day's toil it's a bit of an effort to drag yourself away from the box on a rainy evening to look at wet walls. He hopes you will think 'I'll do it at the weekend.'

Big mistake because time, weather and burglars go together like egg, chips and beans. They like fog or mist and, if they are first floor men, rain is no problem either so don't let your negligence help him through the trellis and gravel minefields. Even if an earthquake is forecast I always do a late prowl every evening to check that gates and doors are shut and no useful burglar's implements are left out. They'll commandeer anything as a ladder or platform – I will be more specific about these improvisations in the chapters on gardens and sheds, garages and cars, where you'll realise how important it is to give all parts of the house and its surrounds the same security rating.

Checking all parts

It is a grave error to make one door battering-ram proof and have the one opposite held up by string because you don't rate it as a special door. The burglar knows where the traditionally weak points of a house are and would tell you that most people consider the front door is superior to the back door. Why? Goodness knows! Maybe it all goes back to the old tradesmen's entrance days.

That's how some people think and their security is shot through before they even start setting up defences, so let's apportion equal importance to all kinds of entries and exits. A hole is a hole wherever it is! Good! Now as the sound of crunching gravel fades we arrive in the age of the active defender, the one who fights back, and the device that was invented to allow Tutankhamen to lie in peace for eternity. The burglar alarm!

A brief history of burglar alarms

Very flattering for a thief to have a device named after him, but the modern robber can call himself extremely lucky indeed that burglar alarms have improved over the millennia. Here's a brief history of why he's still in one piece. Let's go back to about two weeks after Adam and Eve.

In the beginning there wasn't much to steal apart from someone's wife, husband or an apple, but as soon as gold set the standard trouble was on the way. The wealthy couldn't bear to part with it even when dead, so they took it with them, but this of course presented another problem. Tucked up and nicely wrapped in their graves they were in no state to protect the valuables buried with them. This was worrying and a big social problem because lots of gold, chariot wheels, dead horses, chairs and internal organs were essential if you were to impress the gentry on the other side.

Some form of security had to be dreamed up to ensure that the rich dead arrived over there first class and were instantly accepted into high society. This was easier said than done because even though the burial sites were protected, the guards were scared of ghosts, drank heavily and in spite of the jackals howling, fell asleep as soon as it got dark. All a robber had to do was to employ the famous two-sided spade. If he used the back to clock the guard with and the front for digging, he was home and dry. This state of affairs went on for some centuries and the graves were pillaged until a priest came up with a brilliant solution. The curse!

The curse

Priests ran the show and if they felt that they were losing their grip and the public were getting uppity they'd put whatever was going wrong down to a curse from the gods. This shifting of the blame on to someone else always took the heat off the clergy and kept the terrified congregation firmly on its knees, so it didn't require genius to apply the principle elsewhere. Why not glue a really nasty stinker of a curse to a tomb. It was like National Limerick Day or dreaming up a slogan for cornflakes and they came up with dozens along the lines of 'to he who disturbs the sleep of the king shall death come on swift and silent wings!'

I am not suggesting that this would scare off a burglar today, it would have to be something involving income tax, but the curses had a great effect on the masses who eked out their wretched lives sincerely believing that the king was a rich, good-looking god who was moderately concerned about their grinding poverty. The priests jumped up and down because they were banking on the fact that if you were a very religious person you would not even consider shoplifting, never mind try your hand at grave robbing if there was a curse hanging about.

They were 100 per cent correct amongst the faithful, but unfortunately tomb robbers were the Methodists of their day and of a more Free Church persuasion. If the wealthy wanted to have all the things needed in the afterlife – gold bracelets, plates of cakes, etc – that was OK by them and it was very kind of the monarch to have the swag all neatly piled up and stored in one place.

The first heavily cursed tomb was turned over and the robbers went home and looked at each other. Nothing happened so the conclusion from the thief's point of view was that if he didn't erupt in boils the moment he got home then the curse wasn't all it was cracked up to be. After another 963 robberies the priests realised they were on a loser and the curse lost its power. Where to now?

Underground protection

The next protective measure was even more ridiculous and entailed digging long tunnels deep into hillsides. These terminated in a series of reception rooms, food stores for the deceased, furniture, lots of gold, a burial chamber and in extreme cases of daftness, a large boat.

An underground boat takes some beating, but if you consider just how many labourers would be required to dig the complex how could anyone seriously expect that its whereabouts had a cat in hell's chance of remaining secret? You can't kill them all because of the unions and we know for a fact that Egyptians liked beer, so it stands to reason that they must have talked in the local pub.

Some things never change and in another chapter I'll point out the perils of casual talk and gossip over a pint and a dry white wine. These are just as dangerous today as they were 4,000 years ago, the only difference being that the modern robber isn't interested in your grave unless he's an archaeologist.

Pyramids

The height of lunacy was achieved when even more navvies were signed on to build a couple of million tons of stone over the deceased. Pyramids were very impressive and I would love to have one, but not to be buried in. Still the robbers came and went with the swag and I shouldn't be writing this, but they must have been an amazing breed. I have no respect for the man boasting about burgling 14a Herringbone Street, but you would have to listen to the bloke who told you that he'd just turned over the Great Pyramid and was anyone interested in a two ton gold sarcophagus in the pub chariot park?

Things for the priests were looking pretty dicey, and if hiding tombs didn't work then more desperate measures had to be adopted and it now became very personal. The countless tomb robbers who were apprehended on the job would be turned off in public as a lesson to the rest of us, but these popular spectaculars were superseded when some wag came up with a new idea. If a thief set off to turn over a tomb and was never seen again that would be a very strong deterrent to his mates, so a way had to be found to silence those who had actually penetrated the site.

The first burglar alarms

The first crude burglar alarms were invented! The mechanisms were rudimentary and once used couldn't be switched back on, but everything starts from scratch and here's the principle on which they worked.

It was assumed that the thief had smashed his way into the tomb, so the purpose of the various devices was to prevent him from escaping with the goods. How? Quite a problem for the first burglar alarm designer because the tomb might remain untouched for centuries and then one day some verminous devil appears and snatches the lot. The trick was to kill him, but who could live that long to raise the alarm? Nobody, so the solution had to be not 'who' but 'what'. Now we're getting somewhere and after that conclusion was reached it was plain sailing.

Let's rig up a gadget! This now became an ordinary engineering problem and in no time, using the high tech of the day, several solutions were found. They were quite clever and hugely entertaining from the designer's perspective, if a little messy.

The most popular and simplest anti-burglar apparatus incorporated huge slabs of rock placed in such a way that they almost blocked the intruder's path, but not completely. There was just enough room for him and his mates to squeeze through, but in doing so they were compelled to stand on an innocent looking piece of paving. This in actual fact was a delicately balanced fulcrum stone which if moved unsettled the slabs and caused several tons of the local quarry to fall on the robbers and crush them to pulp.

If the intruder came on his own he was still in big trouble for a mini-stone which reacted to the weight of one man waited for him a little further along. Showers of spears activated by similar careless footwork were an alternative to rock falls along with concealed pits full of sharp things smeared with deadly poison. Nice of you to drop in and success at last. The burglar is beaten.

Was it worth it?

You must be joking. It was a total waste of time and effort, with 99 per cent of tombs pillaged as usual.

In spite of this the famous, rich and dead still did not reach the obvious conclusion that it would be a better idea not to be buried with any valuables in the first place. They could put the gold and silver on show somewhere surrounded by bald-headed Nubian slaves and it would have a better chance of staying in the family. No! They still tried to hide valuables and most tombs were robbed within weeks of the internment, some after only a couple of days, and of the ones that remained untouched I suspect that they'd even been forgotten by the robbers which must be a big let down if you are famous, rich and dead.

When you consider the number of people involved in the pomp of a state burial, from the chief priest to the guy who makes the sandwiches, it seems obvious that thefts from hidden tombs could only have been done with the help of someone on the inside. By that I mean someone on the outside of the inside, but wherever they were information always helps as my careless talk chapter will tell you... but not yet!

You and your burglar alarm

The reason I am boring you with this history lesson is that I am trying to emphasise that the more you attempt to conceal your security measures the less chance you have of frightening off the assessor walking past your home. Let him see what he's up against. Marilyn Monroe never hid her strong points so why should you? If the robber is put off it doesn't matter to him. It's not the Olympics where he has to go higher and faster – he's not interested in challenges.

He just wants a quick in and out with no trouble and the sight of a nice, shiny burglar alarm is a strong deterrent. If it is rusty then it's fairly obvious to him that he is looking at a fake, or an alarm that is never used and certainly never serviced. Remember the final extravagant flourish that the service engineer performs as he completes his work on the outside box? They always leave them shiny.

What's available?

There are still some people who regret the passing of the 20 ton burglar alarm slab, but they'd be the devil to clean and look awful in a semi. Today's models are much more reliable, smaller and with a wide variety of types to choose from. You can have your alarm tailored and fitted to your home by a registered professional, or buy an alarm system from a DIY store and fit it yourself. Whichever route you choose you are taking an enormous step forward in domestic safety and security.

You can have the audible alarm with bells ringing loudly and a flashing strobe light, or the quiet one which alerts you and is also messaging the police. There are alarm systems that require wiring in and others operated by electronic pulses but they are all easy to operate.

What's stopping you?

So what is the major obstacle to a mass burglar alarm breakthrough in the UK? Why doesn't every home and office in the British

Isles have a functioning, regularly maintained alarm system? I have put these questions to dozens of people, experts, police and householders and the principal responses are always the same. Cost and the fear of setting off the alarm system accidentally.

Cost

Let me correct you on these misapprehensions immediately. The cost of installing a security system in a four-bed roomed family house is much less than you would lose if you were robbed. It's as simple as that. You have a choice. Feel secure and ask for a reduction in your insurance premiums or take a chance.

We've already read of the nationwide increase in burglaries and in the same way that smokers risk paying more for insurance cover, I am certain that when the current house breaking surge becomes a plague you will be compelled to adequately protect your property. If your defences do not reach a certain standard you will face being refused insurance protection, so please read the chapter on alarms and insurance carefully. It gives you a breakdown of the various systems and how, after making a choice, having a device installed or setting it up yourself and becoming familiar with its operation, you can be totally confident that your home and the people asleep inside it are well protected.

Accidental alarm phobia

This is a common complaint, easily curable and with a little care able to be transmitted to thieves, burglars and other criminals. It is the fear of loud noises in the night accompanied by flashing lights and burly policemen with dogs. It is only right that the crook going about his business should be paralysed by the unexpected racket, but unfortunate for law abiding folk going about their business in bed.

Let's start at the beginning by stating the obvious. If the alarm does go off it is for one of two reasons. An intruder is on your property or it has been set off accidentally. Modern alarm systems do not burst into song unless advised to do so. Faults don't come into the equation because they have fail safe trips to counteract electrical eccentricities and if the apparatus is sick it will tell you with winking lights, not an ear-splitting scream.

If it is a burglar he will be gone at the first blast of sound without having time to steal from you, so even though you feel on edge you have nothing to reproach yourself with. The same applies to the sneaky type of alarm that quietly tells the police that you have a visitor and would they finish their Indian takeaways and come over to collar him. By the time you stumble out of bed they'll be chatting on their radios and he'll have his nose up against a wall, so you're clear on this one too.

Alarm discipline

Sadly it's the next reason that drops you in it, because I'll bet that when you are suddenly woken by the alarm one of your first thoughts is that it has been triggered by accident and it was your fault.

Disarming honesty, but absolutely correct! It is your fault, but that does not mean that you are a bad person. What it does say is that you remembered responsibility but forgot discipline. To use your alarm properly as the powerful deterrent that it is, it requires going back to school and doing things by rote. It means that we have to assimilate a new routine into our lifestyle, like learning to live with the computer all over again only a thousand times less complicated.

It can be done. It will be a chore at first, and then slyly and unobtrusively become a part of your daily life like shopping, getting the kids ready for school or finding no toilet paper in the loo. Remember when only geeks and nerds used personal computers? Now you can even hear the hum of computers in The Valhalla home for the terminally dotty, so what is holding you back from feeling comfortable with a simple device like an intruder alarm?

The Environmental Protection Act

What most concerns the three and a half people who have heard of it is the 1990 Environmental Protection Act covering noise pollution, which states that loud external sound must be shut off within 20 minutes. Do not allow this law to turn you grey. You or a trusted neighbour will have turned the key well within that time. Furthermore the Act is worth its place just to protect us from the guy whose home is powered by a dozen heavy metal groups.

Choice and affordability

The chapter dealing with alarms will astonish you with the variety and sheer ingenuity of the systems, and it all comes down to personal choice and what you can afford. No two homes are the same. Chapter 9 will explain some of the systems and how to have them installed professionally or by yourself.

My recommendation for the typical family home is separate ground and upper floor intrusion systems, so that as you retire for the night you lay your traps behind you. Systems are like cars in that you should buy from a reliable garage or showroom. You can rely on advice from The National Security Inspectorate and the Security Systems and Alarm Inspection Board. They sound like something out of James Bond, but their results are better than his even without the excitement or girls.

Pets

Pets are the bane of alarm users and they always will be if they are allowed to run the house. Any undisciplined pet, whether it is a Jack Russell or an African rhino, is going to cause havoc in an environment where it can do as it pleases. Some years ago this was true of alarms – you could guarantee that a dog would push open the door that is on the circuit or break an infra red beam. Happily this is not the case today, with alarm systems tuned to height and weight parameters. Yes, they've thought of the burglar crawling along the floor at cat height to slip under the radar and in order for the crafty devil to succeed he would have to tickle the scales at under 4 stones.

Nevertheless, however sophisticated your system is the golden rule on pets is obvious and one that every owner knows and not enough observe. Control the brute! Exercise total mastery so that when the alarm is in operation you know where your dog is, and where he can and cannot gain access. It's commonsense, but pets must never be allowed the freedom of the house at night and should be confined in one place with, of course, sufficient space and water to see them through.

You can forget the water if the python sleeps on your bed, but large animals shouldn't be in the house anyway. They are much better at spooking housebreakers outside than in, because once inside the burglar can give the dog a four-course meal to keep him occupied if he feels like it. Conversely if it's two in the morning he's not making much progress out there in the cold, and probably a couple of quid down, if Blackie has treed him and is now tucking into the prime fillet steak he dropped.

Your interior defences

It is a bit chilly out here and I've done my rounds for the night. The wheelie bin, or burglar's platform, is chained well out of reach of any windows and there are no ladders left out. The lights are all working, so it's time to go inside and see if the interior defences need tightening up.

Let's take one last look at the toilet and bathroom windows to check if they're shut. Yes, I know that they are only tiny, but you would be astonished if you watched a house breaker worm his way through an aperture not much bigger than a keyhole. There's a way of doing it with a wriggle of the shoulders and hips and before you know it that's his feet disappearing through the hole. Not tonight! It's a clear evening, the lights are functioning and the gravel is crunching so in we go. Let's use the back door.

The back door

The back door is always considered to be the least respectable of the house entrances, that's why it's at the back and consequently the key is left in the lock just above the thieves' cat flap. When people ignore the vulnerability of the back door it really gets up my nose. It's the ideal entry for the burglar, because it is often left open and if he has to leave at speed he'll have several garden escape routes to pick from.

Into the kitchen

I read of a questionnaire put to experienced burglars serving time, asking them for their opinions on the rooms in a house that they select for the best pickings and none of them mentioned the kitchen. Crafty blighters! They'd hardly give their secrets away if they were still registered practitioners would they? Believe me, the kitchen is the engine room of the house and tells a burglar much of what he wants to know.

The calendar

His first mine of information is attached to the aforementioned, unimportant door and it is called a calendar. The original purpose of the calendar was to designate the days and months of the year, as well as showing us pictures of the Lake District and Scotsmen trying to kill people with bagpipes.

Details are now irrelevant, swamped by a host of notices attached to or scribbled on the calendar, which are meat and drink to a house breaker. They point out that the occupants will all be on holiday in Florida from the end of May to the middle of June which is very helpful. There are several dates and times for doctors and dental appointments, a couple of parties, a barbecue, the theatre and an evening PTA meeting at the school.

There are other notices, but those are the ones that will sting you, so in future when an aide memoire is needed why not use a simple code? Torremolinos won't mind if you call it 'T' and the length of the holiday doesn't have to be shown chronologically. Use signs that mean nothing to an intruder, because the moment he meets any obstruction or delay he will swiftly move on.

The letter rack

His time is precious so let's take a look round the kitchen for that thing I mentioned a while back. Yes, there it is. Our old friend Pedro and he's still bursting with letters, envelopes and assorted scraps of paper holding all the things not worth stealing that we discussed in Chapter 2.

You really must remember to file those deadly bits of paper. A quick shuffle through the scraps makes a meal for a burglar, so in future whenever you buy or sell or receive confidential details from any source put them somewhere safe. If they are no longer pertinent shred, burn or eat them. But make it your business to be certain that they are destroyed.

Handbags

It's not done to shred ladies handbags, so the first lesson with these items is do not leave them downstairs. A bag has money, credit cards, keys, bricks, everything that a woman carries round with her each day. Yet when it's time to retire I guarantee that 90 per cent of women leave their handbags in the kitchen or cloak-room. Men are only slightly less guilty, because they are not expected to take their briefcases to bed, but they also tend to leave bags lying around unattended. Don't do it! If you carry items around all day like a baby, treat them like children.

Keys

Before we leave the kitchen we should rethink our unfortunate habit of labelling the keys hanging or hiding in various rooms. If you can't remember what fits in where and you really need to label, use codes and call the front door Elizabeth II, Dracula or Beckham and you won't be helping the thief.

Come to think of it, if you were really doing the job properly he'd be too far away to read the labels because all of your accessible windows, not just the kitchen but all 93 of them, should have unlabelled, key operated locks. Most burglars gain entry through windows, so tip top security in that area, and deadlocking your outside door, scuppers the great majority of thieves. They will have to trudge elsewhere for pickings.

Don't forget, sentiment is out of the window for the burglar and it should be the same for you. If Mr Smith can't be bothered to go to the trouble that you have embraced that's his lookout! His attitude may change when he becomes a statistic, i.e. one of the British crime survey's estimated 800,000 burglaries each year, or put in a really chilling way, one every 32 seconds.

Locks and bolts

Hard to believe – one quarter of a burglary as you read the fact! That's one each for everyone in England called Popplewell, so stay out of the crowd and fix key operated locks to all of your windows. All outside doors too must have bolts and British standard key operated deadlocks – and if you label the keys I shall send big Arthur around!

If you do see him he will remind you that all the locks in the world are useless if the door to which they are fixed and the frame that holds it is weak or rotten, so give the woodworm exactly two minutes warning and start repairs or replacement. If you have double doors leading to other rooms fit security bolts with removable keys top and bottom and a lock.

Patio doors

If we slip through into the next room it may have patio doors looking out to the garden, or from a burglar's viewpoint looking into your home. This type of door is mounted in a sliding frame, which the thief can lift off its tracks, so locks should be fitted to give an unauthorised Hercules severe doubts regarding his marriageable status.

Insurance implications

So far we've covered windows and doors, but if you are going to the trouble of building a strong defence, let's think for a moment. It would be a shame if your insurance company said 'very impressive,

Miss Thong, but how would someone selling time shares react to your exploding doormat?' If we tighten up on home security our insurers will sing, dance and reduce our premiums, but...

There's always a 'but' and in some cases it is the proviso that the installation of security systems and alarms be carried out by companies registered with the National Approval Council for Security Systems.

You might be happy to go along with this, but if you're into self-help there is absolutely nothing to prohibit you from setting up your own alarm courtesy of your local DIY store. I read recently that DIY is on the ebb – don't you believe it. If you doubt me pop into any big dealer and see the stuff on offer. They wouldn't make it if they couldn't sell it, and the variety of defence measures, professional and amateur, that are available is astonishing. There's a chapter on alarms and what the reasonable insurance companies want in return for reduced premiums coming up.

DIY security

Take a long look and see how you can benefit monetarily and security wise. Plastic anti-climbing spikes and rooms that fill with smoke – you won't believe what is on offer!

It's not all mind-blowingly modern and there are commonsense, simple precautions like this one. Looking out of the front window I am delighted to see that you adopted the American postbox with padlock and consigned the letter box to the dustbin of history. Who wants bent coat hanger fishermen hooking keys via the letter box? The postbox has a narrow aperture to keep eyes and hands out and is well away from the house, so you have eliminated another risk factor.

Lace curtains and window locks would have completed the picture, but you haven't got that far yet and, I'm sorry to say, you haven't photographed and indelibly marked every valuable piece. How do you hope to make an indisputable insurance claim if you have no evidence to substantiate the losses? How would you prove that the items were yours in the unlikely event of them being recovered? Mark and photograph every room and everything that you value.

The hall

If we wander out into the hall we arrive in the deadly dangerous Bermuda triangle. One minute your handbag is there, the next it's gone because this is the distraction crime zone which is defined in law as 'any crime where a falsehood, trick or distraction' is used on the occupant of a dwelling to gain or to try to gain access to the premises to commit burglary.

You'll feel such a mug if you become a victim, the more so because we all know how it's done and are constantly warned about it. The trouble is we think that it only happens to doddering old nitwits who would happily allow Genghis Khan and his Mongol horde into their homes. Not true. Distraction crime is an art form and when a charming young fellow like me is holding your attention at the front door, my thuggish mate is breaking in at the back.

Bogus callers

Why am I explaining something that you all know about? Because people still fall for a bogus caller! I'm tired of saying this, but if someone you don't know knocks at the front door don't admit them. Women are good at this crime, particularly if they are young and pretty, and if ID isn't immediately presented without being requested, ask them to leave. You have a bogus caller.

Put a chain on the front door to prevent a solo thief from snatching the handbags that women tend to leave on the hall table when they come home and the phone's ringing or the dog has to be let out. Remember nobody from the post office, council or a charity will stay if their presence is not required, and if the caller rambles on, close the door and check the rear of your home for forced entry and theft. If in doubt do not receive strangers at the front door and never leave a handbag or valuables close by.

Entrances

Can I have the last word on entrances? Do you know anybody who has a cat flap in their front door? Don't be ridiculous, it would spoil the look of the house and we can't have the whole world knowing that our front door has a gaping hole in it. I agree and my view on holes in doors is that there shouldn't be any – none at all. No cat flaps or letter boxes, because we seem to forget that if you lift the cover of these apertures you can see inside the house (sometimes even the alarm box) and insert your hand or fishing rod to hook keys in the locks.

If you still insist on a cat flap I can only advise you to keep your fingers tightly crossed or hang a severed arm on a length of string outside the back door, remembering to change it every couple of weeks... That is what I think of cat flaps and letter boxes!

The study

If you have a study or office downstairs, as either a business centre or hideaway to sort the household accounts, ensure that it is locked when not in use. When you are wrestling with council tax, or bank and credit card statements, remember that these items in the hands of an identity fraudster can seriously disrupt your life, so put them in a safe place.

My safest place is my safe, which doesn't just sit there looking grey and chunky, but is bolted to the floor. It is approved by the Loss Prevention and Certification Board, LPCB and conforms to European safe testing requirements which specify the amount of money and jewellery guaranteed overnight cash cover.

Desk drawers are fine for blank letterheads and tubes of Polo mints, but personal and financial documents require harder shells. Strong boxes, if they are strong, are good, but only if chained to a fixed point to deny the thief carrying it off to smash open at leisure.

Upstairs

Remember when you made that remark about 'nothing worth stealing in my home'? You know better now so we'll climb the stairs to the treasure room. We're wise to what the thief is after, so apart from switching the landing light on when it's dark we've learned not to leave half of the house unlit when we're watching TV in the Blackpool illuminations of the lounge.

The bedroom looks pretty good now that you have packed your jewels and placed them in the safe. I'm afraid that's where they'll stay until a walk-in safe with dressing table and mirrors comes on the market. When that day arrives you can stop putting the 864 carat Star of Scunthorpe in the vault, but not before.

Security review

You must secure everything that is dear to you, regardless of intrinsic worth, because it is a thieves' market and you cannot relax vigilance. What you see from the inside is a home, but what the miserable wretch slipping through the shadows of Inkerman Road picks up on is a fortress. He hates bright lights and drawn curtains, window snap locks and multi-purpose bolts, mortice deadlocks, sash jammers and hi-tech electronic defence systems. He's not over the moon about fierce dogs either, but if the risk is worth it he can turn Fang into a cuddly toy, so don't depend on your miniature poodle.

Tonight, just before you call the end of play, have a quick scout around and if all is well shout 'goodnight world' and go back in. Switch on the alarm and after a final visit to the loo – who left that blasted window open – you can retire safely.

That is the ideal set-up, but hold on, maybe we are running ahead of ourselves and you don't have a Star Wars security alarm yet? Don't worry. We're getting there and you are 50 times more security minded than you were a few pages ago.

Just to jog your memory here are some dos and don'ts.

Dos and don'ts

- Do add trellis fencing and prickly shrubs to hedges and walls.
- Do close gates. A closed gate says 'no'.
- Do use gravel and passive or activated lighting.
- Don't forget your nightly round of the estate.

- Don't give some doors a lower security value than others and never have a hole, letterbox or a cat flap in an exterior door.

- Don't conceal your security measures. You're not trying to catch the thief, who will only get a slap on the wrist anyway. You just want him to go elsewhere.

- Do see that exterior alarm boxes are clean and look serviced.

- Don't allow fear of setting your alarm off accidentally deter you from having one fitted.

- Don't allow pets the run of the house unless you have a weight and height sensitive alarm system.

- Do keep your wheelie bin or 'burglars' platform' chained away from windows.

- Don't let the kitchen calendar tell a burglar details of holiday dates etc.

- Do file important documents in a safe place, or destroy those forgotten scraps of paper which can cost you your identity and oodles of money.

- Don't label keys. It's as bad as leaving notes in bottles or under the doormat.

- Don't fix a super lock to rotten woodwork in doors and windows.

- Do check with your insurers before installing a security alarm system.

- Do use a postbox with a narrow aperture and secure lock.

- Don't take any notice of what people say about your lace curtains.

- Don't allow a caller you don't know into you home without ID and beware if the caller distracts you while an accomplice steals your possessions.

- Don't forget. Upgraded security means reduced insurance premiums.

chapter 5

Gardens and Sheds

T here are times when I think this world is as gaga as the judges who prefer criminals to paint church halls rather than sending them to jail. I've reached this conclusion because I've known a few crooks, but never met one who preferred prison to community service group painting activities.

A further reason for disillusionment is the sad fact that I have to write a chapter on sheds and garden security. Sheds, for goodness sake! The universal joke hideaway for every Dad where he could smoke, break wind and watch Mrs Hotchkiss hanging out her smalls. He could smuggle his mates around for a sly bevvy, either in his own garden or on the allotment because the shed has its own universe, full of assorted rubbish like broken mowers, paraffin, garden tools and spiders. The only threat came from the weather, kids breaking the windows and Mr Hotchkiss. Not any more!

Shed security

The old sheds were usually ramshackle affairs, teetering on falling over and with buckets placed under the leaking roof, but with the advent of the very posh, easy to erect wooden or plastic structures sheds take on a more glamorous aspect. Thieves who wouldn't normally go near a carton of slug pellets now began to think 'if he's spent anything from £400 upwards on that, and £2.38 on a padlock with a loose hasp, it must be worth a quick inspection!' They were spot on.

Today's sheds in general are more caviar than fish and chips, and often fitted for summer and winter use. They are stuffed with valuable items for the burglar either to steal and sell, or to employ for forced entry into the owner's home, which is a convenient 50 yards distant!

Beat the burglar

The easiest way to prevent a prowler from seeing the goods is so simple it will make your toes curl. How do I stop an intruder taking stock through the windows? Fit blinds! They keep the shed cool and admit light in summer, and when the electric or fluorescent (there's posh for you) light is on at half past three in the afternoon in winter make it difficult for a thief or the lady wife to see what you are up to! When a burglar assesses a shed the first items he looks at are doors and windows and if he sees fitted blinds he will hesitate.

He's off to a bad start and if the door security reminds him of a scene from 'The Birdman of Alcatraz' you will have a thief who appreciates that he is up against someone who really cares, although he will not actually use those words to describe you.

Door security

You are ahead of the game, but only if you ensure that your door padlock is sturdy, and the hasp and base unit is firmly screwed to the door with no signs of 'burglars' delight' – or rust as we call it. Thieves know when security is for show, but never used, so make yours look bright and scratched.

Some people say that sheds are so flimsy today that a thief could lift a plastic one off its foundations and replace it without spilling anything. Sounds flip, but I'll bet they've never tried it. Anyway the purpose of security is not to sell steroids, but to discourage and depress the thief and send him on his way. Every security obstacle means delay, which leads to frustration, clumsiness and worst of all, noise! It doesn't matter if the obstacle weighs a ton or half a kilo, if it makes a noise when the intruder lifts, pushes, kicks or shakes it you have a frightened crook who is on the verge of a quick exit.

A door with two or three locks is as depressing to a robber as one with 50, so impress him. Deadlocks, padlocks, bolts, latches, hooks and chains will leave him wondering about trap doors, and pits and what next?

Hideaway syndrome

On the other hand, if you let him in through negligence the shed, which is more often than not away from the house, allows him to work in splendid isolation and at his own pace. It really is amazing to discover what people keep in sheds and other permanent and semi-permanent garden structures. I wouldn't mind betting that a few thieves have been equally surprised and delighted.

I put this down to 'hideaway syndrome', a reaction in the brain of a man which causes him to see sheds and gardens as havens of peace in a busy world. HS is principally an affliction of men, because while women take on the burden of life just as much or even more than men, their outside efforts seem to be centred more on making the garden look beautiful from a kneeling position.

Men of all ages have the complaint, and the symptoms of advanced tranquillity are sighs of relief and extreme carelessness. That is why the shed we are looking at has no blinds and the door is secured, if I can use the expression, by a padlock which looks closed but isn't because the key was lost in the pond last summer. The two little revolving clamps are doing a great job of holding the door closed, but are absolutely useless against anything more determined than a moth.

Take a look at your shed

What I have just written will probably infuriate you, because your shed isn't like that! Are you sure? I'll bet I could be inside it in seconds, because I guarantee that if you go out and look at it right now you'll find a loose this and a broken that. Don't forget that rust and tiny keys are always being mislaid so be absolutely certain that, never mind what people say, you have shot your bolt and locked the locks.

The fact that two locks are better than one is excruciatingly obvious to me, but for some reason not to millions of shed owners. Why? Surely anything to further delay an intruder after he's spent precious time trying to disable the first line of defence is a major deterrent. Think about it and go double every time.

Next I am going to assume something which I know I shouldn't, but here goes. When you finished yesterday's gardening, wood-work, transcendental meditation, etc you were not too idle or forgetful to put everything you had used back in the shed were you? If you did leave items astray the thief can either steal them or, if they can be adapted to housebreaking, use them to force entry into your home and maybe next door.

That would take some explaining, so save embarrassment and house to house street fighting by doing an evening round of the shed and garden area and if you have left anything out, put it away. If you find nothing you are either becoming security conscious or it has already been nicked. The choice is yours.

What's in a shed?

We've checked the outside, so let's look inside. Which brings us back to Chapter 2, There's Nothing Worth Stealing in My Home! I think you will have been shocked and surprised at the value of the items I pointed out back there and while the garden shed lacks the glamour of the master bedroom with en suite jacuzzi, it still has lots to interest a thief.

Sheds have changed dramatically over the last few years and while the man inside is much the same, the style and size of garden structures make them unrecognisable to anyone over 70. The thief isn't quite so fazed, because he very quickly homes in on the fact that if a potential victim is willing to pay a large amount of money for a garden Taj Mahal, he will still have enough left over to buy valuable items to place in it.

Gardening tools

More space means more sets of expensive hand tools and, as you're wired for power, a juicy selection of costly electrical tools and gadgets all worth a few quid in a car park somewhere. He'll even go for the garden implements and although I haven't yet met a winner of the joint burglar of the month/gardener of the year cup you can be certain that he will steal everything except the horse manure.

People rarely report the theft of gardening kit, but they should because the cost of a stainless steel trenching spade can only be truly appreciated when the victim has to pay for its replacement.

Make time to look around your shed and estimate the cost of replacing the items that used to be fixed to or hanging from the walls. When you reach a figure, sit down and then add the repair bill for the shed damage. That is assuming, of course, that no damage was done to the electric wiring, the tap wasn't left running or the heating switched on to 'kill'.

Bespoke sheds

So far we've only talked about sheds being used as work rooms and rest homes, but as the structures grow bigger they are often put to other uses – private cinemas for the lads, drinking dens, store houses for sports gear and repositories for many kinds of collections and hobbies, some unique and of great value. Some even stand in for observatories and who wants to lose a £5,000 telescope? Whatever use your shed is put to, protect it, because while it is not as personally painful as having your home broken into, it still represents the thief's contempt for those who do not protect what is theirs.

A final check

Nobody is getting into that shed after tonight without a bulldozer, because when my security recommendations are in place it will deter any thief: two or three locks, padlocks, blinds and tools chained for safety. So after a last radar sweep for forgotten tools, ladders and spades we can turn to the garden itself.

The garden

If your back garden adjoins others we can impede the burglar's arrival and escape routes with rose bushes or others of the prickly variety. Trellis fencing is another option, but good neigh-bourliness and discretion affect the issues here, so talk it over with next door and opposite before building the fence.

Nearly every problem in life is a result of misunderstanding or lack of communication, so show the neighbours that you value your property and belongings and infect them with the security bug. If they follow your example, great, if not, it's their look out.

The media regularly cite the UK's worst cities and towns for crime. You may not live in the top three, but things change. The high speed motorways that link our principal centres allow criminals to widen their range and still be home before breakfast, so let's stay on our guard.

Protect your gnome

By referring to long range theft and housebreaking I am not saying that a gang would travel 200 miles just to steal a watering can. I am emphasising the fact that nowhere is exempt from robbery. If you think you are, that breeds carelessness and one day you will find your gnome's mushroom unoccupied and his little fishing rod lying in the grass.

Believe it or not, thieves do steal garden gnomes. They will take or use anything that will help to swell the night's takings. If you haven't left a ladder out for them they will use garden tables as platforms to stand on and reach an open window.

Garden furniture

If your garden furniture is really cheap and nasty, wobbly plastic stuff he will, hopefully climb up on it, fall off and break his leg. That's an unexpected, excellent deterrent and money well spent, but don't try it at home.

At the other end of the scale an expensive oak or wrought iron table will suit him admirably if he can drag it over to the launch pad. I said 'if' because he'll get nowhere if the table is anchored to its site or the chairs are linked to it by chains.

MR. MARSH DEMONSTRATES OUR NEW ANTI-BURGLAR GARDEN FURNITURE!

Do you think precautions like this are fussy and over the top? If you do you are wrong, because your outside furniture tends to sit on the same spot in the garden all summer and you picked that location deliberately. It accommodates you and the sun nicely when the family lunches outside or enjoys a barbecue and you'd be foolish to move it anywhere else. The chains to be used don't necessarily have to be the ones that Brunel liked to be pictured with. That would be picturesque but over the top and any modest chain attached to a fixed weight or metal eye will do the trick.

Wheelie bins and that other back door

The same applies to the menace of the wheelie bin which also doubles as a burglar's table platform. By all means take it for a walk when the waste wagon calls, but at all other times treat it like the Count of Monte Cristo – chained to a dark corner and well out of reach of windows and flat roofs.

The back door that lives next to the bin is another often over-looked security risk. If there was a premier league of entrances it wouldn't be allowed in.

The back door of the house itself comes a distant second to the posh front door, but if you have a narrow alley or side entrance to your home where the bin hides, that back door is held in such contempt that it is usually left on the latch. Nobody bothers to bolt it because it creaks in a light wind and wouldn't stop a – here we go again! The same old wrong reasoning.

For the last time – well, maybe not – your burglar isn't coming in a tank to smash his way in. Ram raiding is a branch of villainy which he thinks is crude and vulgar because he likes to be quick and silent, in and out before they know. Therefore anything which holds and delays him is a deterrent. If it creaks, rattles or sticks it's as bad for a burglar as a row of milk bottles smashing, so bolt the back, lesser, utterly unimportant back door top and bottom, OK?

What else do we have in our garden?

The large heavy items, statues, lawnmowers, etc are usually too much for a one man intrusion, but if the house is empty robbers can pose as gardeners and clean up. In this book there is occasional mention of organised invasions of homes and property involving more than two criminals, but these are not common.

When they do occur the object of the organised type of burglary is either to steal a particular object, or objects such as collections or examples of rare or exotic items: books, birds' eggs, stamps, etc. There's no doubt in my mind that if a collector elects to keep high value, publicised items in their home they really do need watch towers and electric fences. I'm taking it for granted that the koi carp in your small pond is worth less than £5,000 but be sure, even if it's only a £20 fish a thief could take it.

Children's toys

Children's toys are another 'gimme', so each night see that your swings, Wendy houses and bicycles are either locked away or firmly secured. I'm aware that security can be a real pain with the continued checking this and fixing that, but it's still better than looking at an empty space where something that was yours or your children's used to be. That is if you can see the empty space, because if you like those little solar lights that are plonked in the lawn or rockery to make the garden look like Heathrow, the toys will have gone. Although this may not be a bad thing, because picking them up each night is a chore and who wants an air bus parked on the patio?

Dos and don'ts

- Do have blinds in the shed windows, to stop robbers looking in.

- Don't leave tools, garden implements or ladders out at night. Put them away in a secure place.

- Do secure the shed door with more than one lock. Make it look daunting.

- Do be extra vigilant if you keep or store valuable items in the shed. It's common sense, but…

- Don't allow locks and hinges to rust. Check regularly.

- Don't plant prickly bushes or erect high trellis fencing without informing your neighbours. They are all part of the defence team.

- Do be aware that burglars will steal anything from statues to koi carp.

- Do ensure that garden furniture cannot be used as platforms for a burglar to gain first floor entry.

- Do secure the wheelie bin out of range of windows.

- Don't ignore the side back door. Secure it, because one door is as important in defence as another.

- Do put children's toys away at night.

Caution – stay away from this oriental robber.
The Times June 06

This Japanese bank robber gave the game away by asking staff 'any idea how you rob a bank?' The 58 year-old man was armed and planning to hold up the bank in Kumagaya, but obviously had little experience of the task. The bank clerk passed the robber's query to a colleague, who asked him to leave. As he politely complied, the robber accidentally stabbed himself in the leg. He was then arrested for illegal possession of a weapon.

chapter 6

Garages and Cars

For the majority of us the most expensive buy of our life-time is the house we make into our home. Next comes the kids, but if you are lucky you'll be able to push them out of the nest just at the right moment before they overtake the house cost-wise.

Somewhere between the two is the car. The 2.5 litre, twin over-head Clarkson windblaster becomes as intimate a member of the family as the goldfish, but considerably more demanding. It drinks a goldfish under the table and is off sick more regularly, so it needs carefully looking after.

I can't wait to reach the next chapter, which deals with the give-aways and routines that enable thieves to read our life timetable and predict what we'll do next. In it I'm going for the throat of careless, negligent people, not you of course, who throw hand-bags and briefcases on the passenger seat and complain when a traffic light thief strikes. These are what I call 'stop and go' crimes which occur when the car is in city centre traffic or multi-storey car parks and I've given some commonsensical security advice.

Your stationary car

At the present moment, however, we are looking at the car when it is at rest, doing absolutely nothing except depreciate with the speed of light. It sleeps in the garage, but during the day sits on the drive waiting for something to happen. We don't bother to put the car back in the garage after the school run, it's a fag and we'll be using it several times through the day, sometimes in a rush – oh, is it that late?

It also seems a good idea, if mad panics are forecast, to reverse into your drive or parking space. This ensures a smooth, safe exit without the reversing crystals in your vertebrae cracking like sugar on the kitchen floor as the neck attempts an 'exorcist' swivel. Car thieves heartily endorse this homeopathic opinion on reversing disorder and I guarantee that, even if he isn't familiar with your drive, he could exit from it, facing forward and in your car, much faster than you ever will.

Parking prudence

A car facing an exit is much easier to steal, so make it difficult for him. It's your drive and you should know it by now, but if you still insist on reversing in, at least turn your front wheels away from full speed ahead. They don't have to be at right angles to the wheel arch, just leave them a few degrees off centre and you've done enough to cause concern to a thief in an unfamiliar drive and getaway car.

If you forget one morning that you have employed this manoeuvre and the car is going in not quite the direction intended, you'll know how a thief feels. Leave your wheels facing in or out and when you switch on the ignition, whatever you do, don't try to straighten them until the car is moving slowly. Turning the wheels of a motionless vehicle is like you standing barefoot on gravel and attempting to move your feet by twisting your shoulder and waist. It wouldn't do your ankles or the soles of your feet a lot of good and the same applies to your car.

In-car valuables

Don't leave valuables like handbags, briefcases, mobile phones or navigational systems in the beast when it is unattended and always lock it, even in your own drive. If there's a baby visible or advertised as in the car, with the 'small person on board' sign, you should remember that it means absolutely nothing to anyone except a thief because it indicates to a villain that... Do you know? If you haven't got an answer, it's in the next chapter, but just calm down for a moment because we haven't finished here yet.

Bad car habits

The worst thing about bad car habits is that we are totally unaware or deliberately casual about most of them. We don't care and the next chapter on Out and About Giveaways will spotlight some of the outrageously easy challenges we set the thieves and how it is even easier to deprive them of temptation.

We spend so much time in our cars that they become moving chairs with heating, air conditioning and satellite navigation telling us how to get there. We can even call ahead to tell 'em we're on the way as we whiz along listening to Terry Wogan. The problem is that everything connected with the journey, with the exception of Terence, can be stolen from us in a split second or four hours of utter carelessness.

Next time you put the baby in the car just chuck it on the passenger seat so that he bounces once or maybe one and a half times. You know, like you do with your handbag or briefcase! Shocked? Of course you are. It's an appalling suggestion and you would never dream of doing it, but if the image sticks in your mind as you reverse out of your gates tomorrow it means that I'm registering with you. You'll look at the passenger seat with a new respect and I'll be doing really well because I've talked you into seeing things like doors and seats in a completely different light. You'll see that the vase which Uncle Ming gave you shouldn't be rolling around on the passenger seat and at least should be wrapped in a Sainsbury's plastic bag.

If you want to hang on to your car-borne valuables, take careful note of the chapter parked next to this one and own up if you are caught out on any of them.

The garage

It's time to take a look at the garage – or several garages, because we have a choice.

There's the lock-up, which you can see but is out of reach if a yob is disfiguring it with graffiti, and there's the garage that is part of the house with a connecting door. The car port doesn't figure in the equation as it is open, and unless there's a brick on the plastic roof, defenceless. So the final alternative is something that looks like a World War Two air raid shelter. It is the lonely detached garage.

In defence of the garage

One thing such different structures have in common is that we can employ the same first line of defence in each of them.

The garage defender
The garage defender is a hinged, metal bollard sunk into the ground in front of the door which can be locked in raised or lowered mode. When it is standing proud it will prevent the garage doors being opened by thieves and make the taking of a vehicle an extremely difficult and noisy exercise.

Locks

You can confound them further with a central bolt on the doors which denies to the thief that vital fraction of movement and slack that he hopes to either push back and forward or jam a jemmy into.

Again I remind you, more locks are better than one, but they must be the correct kind of locks. More combination locks are not necessarily better than one and the same applies to cylinder type locks. Most locks can be got at, that is they have an aperture or gap into which a skilled operator can insert a sliver of plastic or metal and in a matter of seconds – click – come on in!

Thanks, but no thanks. I prefer deadlocks which are exactly what they say they are. Once a deadlock is in position it is inert and no amount of coaxing will shift it out of its groove unless the thief has a 200 ton electromagnet at his disposal.

Next time you are in your local DIY store make time to do a lock inspection tour and look at the wide variety of security devices on display. You'll find that in our hi-tech age of infra-red beams, and motion and heat detectors, some of the oldest and simplest devices still hold their own. Any simple method of defence like a sturdy deadlock or length of chain that has survived this long must be pretty good. As ever place some of your locks above kicking height and see that they look bright and rust-free.

If the garage has wooden window frames check that the putty hasn't reached pensionable age and is ready to be picked out with a sharp tool or even a finger. Any window covered in cobwebs, and unopened since Dunkirk, suggests to a thief that it is an unvisited, weak point and a potential way in.

Inside the garage

Once inside the garage, the robber can take stock. Garages are usually full of cars, tins of paint, power tools and other electrical gadgets, but to me the semi-detached garage offers a much greater opportunity to a thief than nicking batteries or power drills.

The connecting door

It is the chance to use the connecting door leading directly from the garage straight into the domestic area. This door is another source of amused bafflement to a reformed burglar, because nine times out of ten, due to its classification as an interior door, it has panels you could blow through. This is another great forgotten door, not quite so disreputable as the one outside by the wheelie bin, but critical. People forget that if your outer garage security is not up to scratch, this door becomes absolutely redundant.

You mustn't discount the connecting door just because it leads into the pantry, cloak or washroom. I know such places have no dramatic standing in the hierarchy of rooms, but the average burglar is not a snob and will slip through any kind of door that may lead him to your valuables.

Garage duties

There's something odd about a garage in that it is one of those buildings that doesn't belong to its parent house, but neither is it a shed so the question is, who is directly responsible for its security?

Without hesitation most women will say 'his' because garages, like sheds, are masculine. I can't quite follow this line of reasoning and while I admit that kitchens and bedrooms are feminine, the lady of the house may use the car as much as or more than the man, so where does that leave us? You can sort that out amongst yourselves but I only bring up this 'his 'n' hers' argument for security purposes.

If it is a woman in charge of the garage the chances are that it will be clean and orderly. If dad rules it is more likely to be a shambles of boxes, old furniture and junk, a minefield that a burglar would have to hack a path through to reach the expensive tools and connecting door. It looks like a win for the boys and you could come back from your holidays to find a burglar trapped and convalescing with a broken leg under that woodwormy old Welsh dresser that fell on him. Sounds good, but I'll tell you why it isn't.

If an intruder broke into the garage through your negligence, I can assure you that even in extreme pain and on oxygen he would somehow crawl to the connecting door on a 98 per cent certainty that a sharp kick on one of the panels with his good leg would knock it out. It's not hers and it's not his sole responsibility for security, it's ours, so go and look at your connecting door and tap the panels with your fist. You'll know if the resonance is strong or feeble. If they shiver hang a heavier door with panels that feel like part of the door's ribs, not its spare tyre.

Dos and don'ts

- Don't throw handbags, briefcases, Ming vases or babies onto the passenger seat.

- Do not reverse into your drive. A car thief is happier going forward in an unfamiliar drive.

- Do park with wheels turned left or right, not straight ahead.

- Don't try to turn the steering wheel when the vehicle is stationary.

- Don't leave navigational systems, phones, etc in an unattended vehicle.

- Do lock your car even when you can see it out of the front window.

- Do ask your dealer about tracker devices in cars and their installation.

- Do install a garage defender bollard to prevent a thief leaving the garage in your car with your television set.

- Do install extra locks, deadlocks and bolts on garage doors.

- Don't allow garage window frames made of wood to rot, or the putty seal to crack or disintegrate.

- Do ensure that the vitally important house/garage connecting door is sturdy with solid panels.

- Don't advertise 'small person on board' to a thief. This could mean an unlocked car or open windows because of an infant passenger.

- Don't treat the garage as any less important than the home. It's a thief's way in!

chapter 7
Out and About Giveaways

Some people never give up sucking their thumbs. It is probably the earliest habit we pick up and it is the forerunner of many more that we will adopt in our lifetime. Without the safety of habit we would lose track of our responsibilities and obligations, but on the debit side if we are slaves to ritual and routine we become boringly predictable.

If a robbery victim has been done over because a thief locked on to a routine that he read like a book, the feeling of outrage and embarrassment is doubled.

Routine review

We cannot survive without adhering to various sets of routines. The general pace of life today forces us into dividing the hours into recognisable slots for work, play, family and privacy. This is the way we face each day and if everyone on the planet was as honest as you are our rituals would never place us at risk. Sadly in our present disorderly environment thieves feast on schedules and programmes, and the more rigidly we stick to the day's running order the less secure our homes and persons become.

It is very difficult, and sometimes not feasible, to give up an ingrained habit, so I want to take the easier path of asking you simply to be aware of your routines and find ways to vary them. Nothing as drastic as wearing a false beard to the office or wandering naked through Tesco, but changing the daily pattern of your life just enough to confound the thief who thinks he has sussed you. Yet again it is not a great deal more than being aware of situations and their perils and adjusting your reaction.

Family patterns

No parent will need telling that running a family is impossible without some kind of organisation. If the same skills and the odd threat required to prise three children out of bed, feed them and take them to school each day were applied to the rest of our lives we'd have nothing to worry about. It usually starts to go wrong with that huge sigh of relief when Dad's gone to work and the kids have been swallowed by school.

The school run

In fact the cracks begin to appear just before that moment of sublime joy. To be absolutely precise the whole edifice shatters at 0835 in almost every home in the UK. This is when he goes that way to work, she goes this way to school with the kids and the thief fills in the empty space they left behind in the kitchen. He's got a watch like everyone else, and he could end up with both of yours if you don't look at the Richter scale of your predictability and give it a little earth tremor every now and then.

School time is universal chaos. If it wasn't you would be seriously concerned that there was something very wrong with your little darlings, but it is and you have a tight schedule to shoehorn them into. On alternate days you take your friend's kids to school as well. You are duty driver Monday, Wednesday and Friday and then each month you switch to Tuesday and Thursday.

How do I know that? I've been watching the morning rush and I know that your home is unoccupied for 25 minutes between

0840 and just after 0900. In that time I could take your piano, so the answer is to vary the school run ritual. Check with your friend the day before and ask if she'd like you to go out of synch for a change and do the honours tomorrow instead of the next day. If it's inconvenient, fine, but it will waken her up to the threat of daytime house theft and I'm delighted because now we have two people on a security kick.

School events

What other educational rails do you run on in a straight line and dead on time? There are endless, well publicised school functions and fund-raising events - concerts, swimming galas, prize giving, sports day, term assessments, the dreaded PTA meetings, and mid-term assessments and reports. Everyone knows that they are taking place and even if Dad and the other dads find many of the events distinctly unappealing they are going to be dragged along to them, like it or not. Make a note of that, Jimmy. School play on the17th. Empty house!

Thinking ahead

If you are going to a local event that you know will be well attended you can be certain that it has been equally well advertised. Thieves read the papers too, so if you are leaving your home unoccupied ensure that all of your security walls are up and ask a neighbour to keep an eye on the property.

Breaking the habit

I hope that by now you are allowing your thoughts to wander through other parts of the timetable which controls your daily routine from school to bedtime.

Church

Sunday church service timings haven't altered much over the last 2,000 years, so your religious beliefs can land you in the cart unless there are heathens in the family who stay home. Thieves, like vicars, work on a Sunday, but not to the same standards so leave your home secure.

Shopping

Late-night shopping for people with long working hours is a recent innovation and means that homes are unoccupied at the most unlikely times. Thieves were momentarily thrown off kilter by this commercial ploy, but they soon saw the advantages of either breaking into the shopper's home or meeting her at the supermarket and stealing her handbag. Don't fall into the habit of doing your late night shopping at the same time on the same day every week. Go a little earlier or later. It really doesn't matter which, as long as you step out of the rut and become outrageously unpredictable.

Check your habits

Do you go to Anton's the hairdresser every Saturday at 10.30, or the leisure centre for a workout and light lunch on a Wednesday regular as clockwork? The demands of modern living have reduced the number of stay-at-home women and large numbers of residences are left unoccupied and minimally defended while an individual, single parent or both partners are out at either part- or full-time work. This helps the thief as he knows that houses are likely to be vacant at school drop-off and pick-up time, and in some cases for a considerable time before and after those slots. He will reconnoitre a chosen area rich in young couples and take in the scene as the 4X4s and Chelsea tractors fly by with a waving hand sticking out of the driver's window.

In some cases there are two journeys to start the day, when the old man has to be taken to the station, which gives a house-breaker even more opportunity. And to date we've only discussed cars when they are on the move – the ones that take us to school, work, the leisure centre, hairdresser, church, shopping, the club, soccer, rugby matches and regular coffee mornings in aid of the incompetent burglar's charity. Incompetent? That's all he'll have to be if you stick to your regular routines as punctually as you are doing, because he'll be retired by the time he's 30.

The antidote to bad habits is to look at yourself and, if you see a predictable pattern developing, it will show itself when you begin to feel bored with the same thing. Alter it in small but subtle ways. There are a million clichés about change doing you good and most of them are true. There is however another small drawback.

Habits within habits

There are habits within habits! You can follow my advice to the letter, and do all the major daily routine alterations to beat the thief and somehow completely forget the little changes that he is hoping you would overlook. So far we've only examined those habits which after a moment's thought make you smile and ruefully confess to. Think about them and make the necessary alterations.

Cars on the move

Now it is time to go back to car habits. You, sir, the man who always leaves his briefcase and mobile phone on the passenger seat during and after you have filled up at the garage. And what do you think will happen to that priceless satellite navigational system which talks you out of all kinds of trouble, but is only stuck to the windscreen by a rubber suction cap?

You, madam, place your handbag where he leaves his briefcase. Have you forgotten that thieves hovering at traffic lights pounce like lightning? An arm through the open window or a door ripped open and your belongings have gone. It's a nasty and shocking experience, but it won't happen if you take heed of what I am about to say.

Changing driving habits

Ladies, use your central locking at traffic lights or where any kind of delay causes you to stop for a length of time. If there are bags of any kind on the passenger seat loop the seatbelt through the bag handles and click it into its slot.

The bags, as you well know, shouldn't be there anyway. Their proper place is in the boot, but we are always in a rush so we just sling them in and drive off. If they are seat belted however there is an added, mischievous bonus in the event of a raid. The sneak thief who grabs the bag and exits sharply will be about 18 inches away from the car when the inertia slack of the seat belt is suddenly taken up, crash tight, and he either drops the item or attends hospital with a dislocated shoulder. He has no option other than to retire, so you wind your bag in and drive off.

Children in cars

Thieves know that we don't put our children in the boot and that if they see a young child in a car it is bound to be unlocked. Mum has just popped in somewhere and will only be gone for two seconds, which is approximately one second longer than a thief will need to steal any items left in view.

Take the baby with you and lock the car. Children can be a great distraction inside and outside the home and many parents have to carry their infants with them wherever they go. This is a tremendous strain on a (usually) mother's attention, and with all that is swirling around her on a shopping expedition to the supermarket or shopping centre her first concern will always be the safety and wellbeing of her child.

I can't imagine how anyone can look after two or even three children simultaneously in these circumstances, but I am absolutely certain that their vigilance barometer starts to drop. It is totally understandable and forgivable, but thieves aren't usually of an understanding and forgiving nature, and they know when and where to hit.

With the car parked and the ritual of restraining one child from running off and carrying the other, or jamming it into a pram or pushchair accomplished, the relief to actually get into the supermarket must be palpable. This is how it appears to a man, but women seem to cope somehow. Once inside she will look for the trolley with a baby seat and a hook to hang her handbag.

Bag security

The handbag hook is another great idea that would work fantastically well in a convent, where a hoodie with a different type of hood would stick out like a sore thumb. This, however, is a busy supermarket and the hook is a thief's delight. It is equally convenient for a shopper, but in that split second when Mum spots something on the other side of the aisle, or her child is about to smash a bottle of tomato ketchup, the handbag can disappear.

Carry your bag with you and if it makes you feel safer keep it to your front rather than slung over your shoulder. Shopping is good therapy for harassed wives, mothers and working girls though it usually has the opposite effect on men. Thieves are aware of the relaxation in vigilance, so don't let the euphoria of finding lumpfish roe at £1.50 a jar divert your attention from your handbag. This item has just been carefully lifted from its hook on the trolley by a young man strolling towards the exit or who may even have the cheek to go through the 'nine items or less' checkout!

Stopping thieves reading your habits

The number of occasions when firmly established habits weaken our defences is considerable, but as long as you are aware that today or tonight we are doing something that we, the family, the team, the school and the church always do on this date, you can fight off the thief.

A good method of stirring your memory is to go starry-eyed and nostalgic and say to him, her or them, 'how many times have we gathered in the car park on this date and burned a traffic warden at the stake? It can't be! Is it really ten years?' Then you'll remember that you always leave the house on its own on bonfire night, local and general elections and school functions. You go to the local rugby, soccer and cricket matches by clockwork. You always take your holiday at the same time every year and you visit the grandparents every Thursday, and there's the Monday stint at the hospice... and so it goes on.

There are dozens of set pieces in our lives, which we stick to because when other things go pear-shaped the regular patterns help us to keep a proper perspective on events. Habits are like every other characteristic of human conduct in that some are good and others can be bad, and it is not my purpose to intrude into personal mores or what you get up to in the privacy of your own body. If you steal the vicar's underwear off the washing line, or wear a false beard in bed, then go ahead and I will only poke my nose into your affairs if I think that by carrying on in a particular manner you are unwittingly encouraging housebreakers and burglars.

This is the entire point of the chapter on habits. We encourage the sneak thief, the housebreaker and the burglar unknowingly because we are comfortable in our routines. We adopt them because they make our lives flow more easily, but remember that the joke where you can see the punch line coming a mile away is flawed. You have sussed it because you have heard it several times before and you knew what to expect, so don't allow the thief to read your habits like a bad joke.

Dos and don'ts

▪ Do vary the duty driver programme to school. If you share the school run with a neighbour alter the schedule every couple of weeks so that a watcher will lose track of who is where and when.

■ Don't leave the house at exactly the same time each school or work day. Try an early start for a couple of days and then after a while a later one.

■ Do beware of constantly repeated functions where you leave home and return at the same time. These can be visits to the hairdresser, coffee mornings, work-outs at the leisure centre and attending local amateur sports events which nearly always take place on a Saturday or Sunday afternoon. Professional games mean a three to four hour absence from home on any day of the week.

■ Don't forget the events which occur regularly. These are usually big shows like bonfire night, local and general elections, and Christmas and New Year.

■ Do be on your guard in crowded malls and supermarkets. Finding bargains and working to a budget is hard enough without having children and a thief in tow!

■ Don't hang your handbag on the trolley hook. You will not realise that it has gone until you are standing red-faced in front of the checkout girl with a line of impatient fellow customers piling up behind you.

■ Don't leave the car's navigational system, which has saved you lots of headaches, in the vehicle if it is unattended. It is only fixed with a suction cup, so detach it from the windscreen and place it along with any other valuables in the boot. Satellite navigational systems are highly prized aids in today's traffic racing and can be sold on with the minimum of fuss.

■ Do pay attention to my advice, but if you are still resisting commonsense, and insist on throwing handbags and briefcases onto the passenger seat, the best precaution you can take is to thread the seat belt through the handles or straps and anchor the clip in its slot.

■ Don't forget to use your central locking when held up at traffic lights, or delayed for longer than you would like. Close your windows.

■ Do remember that predictability is the thief's guide book.

It's not all bad news! *The Independent* May 06

Stargazer falls down chimney! Brawley, California (it's always California). A man who was found stuck in a chimney claimed that he had fallen in after climbing on the roof to look at the stars. Police saw differently and arrested him on suspicion of burglary. The 27 year-old man had been stuck near the bottom of the chimney and had to summon help by removing his trousers and waving them around to set off the home's motion detectors.

chapter 8
Careless Talk

At the beginning of World War Two, after stories had started to circulate that the cunning Germans were dropping parachutists dressed as nuns in Holland, a wild fizz of spy mania frothed up in Britain. After a while, when people realised that if the third Reich was that religious the next airborne assault should have consisted of bishops, bell ringers and choirboys, and it didn't, things slowly began to settle down. It then became clear that it was just another propaganda ploy by the government to keep everyone wired up and on their toes.

A tale of careless talk

The whole thing was a godsend to cartoonists, but after a while the theme became stale. When the 'phoney war' settled in, a longish period when not a lot happened, the spy thing went off the boil. This falling off in enthusiasm did not please Mr Churchill, who was as much concerned about security as I am, and he demanded that the Ministry of Keeping Ordinary People on the Hop come up with something less ridiculous, but interesting enough to stick in the wartime public's mind.

The nun's chorus turned out to be a joke, but when the laughter died down the security problem still existed. An enemy you laugh at rather than fear is good for morale, but there is the other face of espionage in wartime. It is the danger of people in the know putting the lives of others in danger by inadvertently disclosing important information over drinks and pillows. A way had to be found to make everyone aware of such carelessness.

Careless talk costs lives

Linking a new campaign with both humour and a serious message, the campaign was a series of drawings all headed with the caption 'careless talk costs lives!' The artwork was light and economical and portrayed everyday scenes in wartime, but with an added ingredient. We would see two sailors chatting in a pub, or an officer and his girlfriend having dinner at the Ritz. Other themes were soldiers in conversation on a train, a couple of women munitions workers having a cup of tea, country gents looking over a fence by a sign saying 'secret!' and an RAF wing commander with a flowing moustache trying to impress a pretty shop assistant.

Nothing exceptional, except that Hitler would be drawn sitting in the seat behind or reading a newspaper at the next table. The sight of him as a waiter, porter, nurse or farmhand on posters and newspapers all over the British Isles at first made people smile, then think. After a while 'careless talk costs lives' slipped into the language, civilians and servicemen did become aware of the dangers of loose comment and that is what this long preamble to this chapter is all about!

The spy in the pub

We still have spies – the big-time international agents who betray their country, the ones who ferret out commercial secrets, and right down at the bottom of the list, the listening burglar and his mate in the pub. Don't however allow his humble position in the league to fool you, because if he is nabbed, instead of several life sentences he has a one in eight chance of just being cautioned. That statistic can't help but make housebreakers feel cocky, and if he can benefit from careless talk it saves him a lot of time and effort. So without becoming paranoid please remember, when in conversation engage the brain before the tongue!

I appreciate that I am talking from experience, while you are at the learning stage, so take it easy and enjoy the Sunday dinner without considering where an individual pea comes from. By that I mean you should concentrate on situations, not detail! The moment a situation takes you over – the music in a supermarket, chatter in a pub, the smells in a restaurant or foreign language spoken on your holiday – it will be then that the associated security precautions that I have mentioned will pop up in your mind like daisies on a newly mown lawn!

Staying aware

I know that if I'm in the hairdressers the conversation will inevitably swing round to holiday times and dates. If it's the pub then the talk will be of tables at sporting dinners which need filling and are you free on the17th? Every location has its perils, but if you can pair up the situation and the danger attached to it you'll have time to think. If you remember the basic commandments you will win that day's security battle.

I keep going on about awareness, but it is as important as crossing a busy road safely on foot. We know what is at stake if we tangle with an HGV, so even strolling along chatting with a friend, the moment we reach a zebra crossing, or decide to make a suicide dash across four lanes of traffic to catch a taxi, we switch to alert mode. Check and when it's safe, cross and on the other side slip quietly back into standby attitude. This is an exercise that has been drummed into us for years and has become automatic. If you apply the same discipline to home security as you do on the high street, you'll be safe from buses, hay carts, slurry wagons and burglars.

The last thing I want to do is to talk down to people about protecting your home and yourself, but I became so irritated when I met prospective victims in my TV series who were totally confident that their home with its minimal protection was an impregnable fortress. Ten minutes later I'm in and out with their fierce dog licking my face before they've finished emptying the bins!

Holiday talk

'We're off to Spain at the end of the month!' You deserve a break and the whole family is really looking forward to two weeks of sunshine, swimming, ice cream and the odd cockroach. How many times have you overheard that in a pub – and not just the pub? The kids are excited and tell everyone at school. While you can't stop them talking, and as yet apprentice housebreakers do not start practising till they are at least 8 years old, you have to live with this lapse of security, but an older brother doing time can be bad news and further reason for strengthening your defences.

If you have noticed that policemen are getting younger these days apply the same observation to burglars and remember to keep even the smallest window in your home closed when the property is unoccupied! We have to forgive the juveniles who talk carelessly, but adults should know better so let's take an in-depth look at the walls that have ears and jemmies.

Pubs are public

We will begin by admitting that most men and some women talk much more when they are slightly oiled. In a convivial atmosphere like that at the Psychopath and Artichoke we positively shine! This is such a cracking pub that along with its large regular clientele there is also a thriving passing trade, and in such a jolly crowd we can relax and lay down the law on sport, politics and sex with every fear of contradiction but no trouble.

We never give a thought to the fact that some person, other than the one we are addressing, is taking in what is being said. Why should we? There are always new faces in the hurly burly at the bar and the place has a great reputation, not like the One Eyed Dog down the road – what a thieves kitchen – throw a few notes around and after the Old Bill's been and gone the DVDs and fridges are lined up in the car park. Wouldn't be seen dead in a dump like that!

Walls have ears

That's an interesting point – you've never been in the Dog and nothing will ever drag you through its doors so you have no idea what the pond life that frequents the place looks like. That man resting his ear on your friend's shoulder as you dish out precise details of the Torremolinos troop movement might be the King of Thieves himself. Here again the passwords are 'aware' and 'caution', because even though the low ceiling raises normal discourse to a roar and you can't hear yourself think, if you point your radar in a particular direction it is amazing what you can pick up. Try listening in on a private conversation for a couple of seconds and you'll see what I mean.

Public houses, however good, bad or indifferent, are major information gathering centres for criminals and the police, so as you enjoy your pint or white wine consider what you are saying and to whom. Fortunately in many pubs bad eggs are either obvious or not encouraged, but as the yob leaves, the damage may already have been done if he's read the notice board. If he knows who is in the darts or domino team, and they are playing an away game on Tuesday and Charlie's wife always accompanies him, that leaves the house empty.

The fewer people who know that a home is unoccupied the better, but if it is unavoidable then it's commonsense to see that every window, door and gate is closed and the alarm set. Of course it is commonsense, but people still don't use theirs.

Drinking, driving and security

While we are at the pub it should go without saying that drinking, driving and security are strangers. If you are over the top as you totter into the dimly lit car park you are a pushover for personal and car theft. Your wallet gone, a sore head, the satellite navigation system ripped out, and if they are in a frisky mood they'll take the car and way out, deep in bandit country, they'll torch it.

Why does the victim next morning cringe in front of a weary police officer and say 'I was a fool!' and then get a nuclear blast from his better half? Because you are human and make mistakes, but you can cut down on these errors and omissions by remembering my advice.

Shopping security

Women don't behave like that in pubs (do they?), but they can be as bad as men when let loose in supermarkets, hairdressers and shops. It is well worth a deadbeat spending ten pence on a tin of beans if he can load his trolley with eavesdroppings of parties, barbecues, holidays and visits to the leisure centre. Here again, I don't want you to stop gossiping, rumour mongering or slandering your friends.

What I do insist on is that when you bandy personal and intimate information do so in a manner that keeps the details confidential! I have to admit that I get as much fun as anyone out of tearing people's characters to bits, but believe me I only indulge when it is safe to do so. I check if anyone is loitering or hovering a little too closely, and if there is anyone who appears to be overly interested in the private life under the spotlight I either change the subject or make it clear that outside interest is not appreciated.

In the case of a woman who believes she is under unwelcome scrutiny by another shopper she should immediately call for the manager of the establishment. It may come to nothing and loud protestations of character defamation, but if the person who is the cause of the trouble makes a fuss he knows his face will have registered with you, the management, and staff and his career as a sniffer in this supermarket will have ended.

Conversely if he leaves without protesting his innocence or waving goodbye he still comes unstuck, because if your accusation was a whimsical one he should be incandescent with rage. If he leaves as quiet as a mouse there's even less chance of him being forgotten, so you should feel pleased. Not only have you rid yourself of a menace, but you have probably saved other indiscreet shoppers. See what happens when you listen to me!

Sharing security concerns

That's men and women dealt with separately, but we can be just as lethal sharing joint security blunders. Any short- or long-term absence from home means a round of cancellings – the newspapers, mail, milk, parish magazine, Playboy and any other kind of regular delivery to the front door.

Anything over two weeks screams of holiday and stoppages of that duration deserve a little more than a risky handwritten note under the mat. Even if you have been especially considerate and tucked it into a milk bottle, and it is in colour with kisses on the bottom, you are asking for big trouble. Do not leave notes, they are deadly dangerous and if you are that careless why not use the paper to write personally to the nearest burglar, giving him directions?

 If you have instructions for the postman, milkman, newsagent or rat catcher give them face to face. I know it's a chore and the postman, unless you know him well, will give you a form to fill in, but it's worth the trouble.

Notifying the police

In the old days we always notified the police of absences from home, but I am not so sure of this practice today. It's not that I don't trust the law, but an occasional sweep by a police car when they are free from collaring binge drinkers and deciding which emergency call comes first in the statistical tangle isn't going to do a great deal for security. It also means that a dozen more people know that your home is sitting there empty.

The same goes if the place is safely guarded. If your home is protected and the mug next door isn't, and he gets turned over while you are away, you are likely to meet some frosty faces on your return. He'll want to know why the cops were there for you and not for him.

Who to talk to

The milkman

Sadly, not many people have doorstep milk today which is a shame because the milkman was often the only contact many old folk had with the world. On the other hand if you buy your milk from Tesco you don't have to tell them that you are going away for a couple of weeks. If you do still live in what the kids call the Stone Age, tell the milkman personally.

The newsagent

Of all the personnel involved in the empty space we leave behind us in June, July and August my strongest trust is placed in Mr Patel the newsagent. My gut feeling is that of all the people with whom we come into contact and who can really hurt us, the newsagent finishes last on the list. I know where he is coming from and this is important because it is not something that can be said about everyone.

Taxi drivers

Taxi drivers cause me concern. Obviously not the ones who are known to you personally, but the casual car you order so that you can go out and have a drink without worrying about the breathalyser. Of these I would say 99 per cent are totally trustworthy and enjoy a good over-the-shoulder chat during the journey.

It is the one per cent that can wreck your day and it doesn't need a car crash to do it.

There are dishonest taxi drivers and we select them by picking up the telephone book or by calling a number from a card pinned to the wall in the pub. We don't make exhaustive enquiries about the driver who is coming to pick us up and take us to the airport or station. Why should we ask for details of his CV, experience, qualifications, safety record, any previous, etc?

There is no need to because the vast majority of taxi drivers are ordinary, decent people earning a crust in a job which swings from exciting to dangerous most Saturday nights and causes terminal frustration during weekday traffic. Unfortunately it's the tiny group of flies in the ointment who spoil the name of cabbie, because while you know for sure that Mr Patel is a newsagent and Charlie the postman is as sick of junk mail as you are and dreams of delivering a real letter one day, you do not know what your driver is or has been in the past.

The taxi driver as stranger

When he comes to the house he is almost certain to be someone you have never seen before, yet you are telling him that your home will be unoccupied for the next couple of weeks! By using a cab you have saved maybe £80 airport parking, but if your home is not secure you have left yourself wide open. Can there be a let down as crushing as coming home bronzed and shiny and opening the door to a house clearance? Dishonest taxi drivers know where you live, where you are going and when you are coming back, information worth a few quid to a burglar and even usable by the driver himself if he dabbles in house-breaking. How do we stop him? It's easy and when you think about it, nothing more than commonsense!

Avoiding trouble

You book your cab giving the date and time you want him to show up, but not the precise address. If it's a road, street, avenue, close or whatever, give him Dingle Street or Church Lane, but not the number. Pick a landmark and be out there to welcome him along with your bags. It doesn't have to be a great distance from your home and if there are no distinguishing landmarks, trees, street lights, etc stand with your bags between two houses. Tough if it's raining, but he won't have a target to pinpoint.

You can make life even more difficult for the crook if you only book the outward journey. To prevent the duration of your absence being known arrange with a friend to book the airport or station return pick-up on the morning of your arrival or, if it is later, at the last minute.

These simple tactics deny a thief the comfort of time and if he feels rushed he'll go on to more leisurely pastures. And don't spoil everything by writing your address on the suitcase labels. More of that later.

Staying sharp

As you read on through the maze of defences and threats there will be a growing rage inside you and you'll want to scream 'what alternative do I have? When I look at the pasty faces around the bar is it wrong to feel a buzz as I tell them that we are off to Los Angeles next week!' I fully understand your feelings and unless you are an admirer of Lord Lucan you don't really want to disappear off the face of the earth, but the point that I continue to stress is awareness. Always be aware.

It is very difficult to be sharp all of the time, particularly with diversions beyond your control like engagements, weddings, christenings, barmitzvahs and funerals. They bring happiness or grief, but what they always cause is chaos and lack of attention.

Some burglars may even be of a religious bent and the place for them to look for information is where they worship. It doesn't matter whether we are talking about High Church, Catholic, Protestant, Methodist or the Tin Tabernacle, they can rely on forthcoming events, hatches, matches and dispatches to be announced well in advance and giving ample time for a leisurely reconnaissance. It's a safe bet that the Smith family will not be its usual ordered self on the day when daughter Kirsty marries Gary, and if you've told the local paper about the service to commemorate Uncle John's selfless years of service to the British Legion... and so it goes on.

The drugs trade

Horrible, isn't it? Things and practices that we took for granted as both private and public, harmless, pleasing and respectful are now used against us and we are exposed to jackals who RSVP with a broken window or a muddy footprint.

That, I am afraid, is the way the world is today and most of the disorder can be put down, without a shadow of a doubt, to the blossoming drugs trade. Usually in a bull market overwhelming demand means an increase in cost, but it has worked the other way in the death trade. What could only be purchased by the wealthy pop star or socialite is now available to all and in some cases is offered gratis to hook another victim.

The Court of Human Rights

The nightmare increase in housebreaking can also be tied up with the increasing encroachment on law enforcement by the Court of Human Rights and its baffling judgements. Each day we read about another instance where a crook attacking someone with intent to rob was apprehended by a policeman. In the resulting scuffle he sustained injuries which necessitated three stitches in his head. When he returned home he told his mother who then found a solicitor willing to sue the police officer concerned.

Reports like this leave most of us, who can distinguish clearly between right and wrong, totally confused. The public would feel even worse if they were aware that some police forces are advised not to chase joy riders in a stolen vehicle. Let 'em go!

Don't give up! If criminals know their human rights more than you do yours then close in on yourself and say that you will guard what is yours and, if they don't like it, try somewhere else. Laws on human rights were not meant to make the work of the police harder and sometimes impossible, but they do and because of this, responsibility for our own security is slowly being nudged further and further into our own hands. Take it.

Establishing your rights

We are not allowed to attack the burglar inside or outside our own homes, except in special circumstances, and while these may be difficult to establish at three in the morning with a hooded figure screaming at you, we are only allowed to use reasonable force. An ex-chief constable of the Metropolitan Police thinks that the rules of engagement with burglars should be changed to give the victim more leeway to flatten the intruder, whether he is coming or going, and most sensible people are in favour of the recommendation.

It is interesting to note that the reason we are not allowed to keep a Kalashnikov in the bedroom and use it against an intruder goes back to the days when some wretch living in a wattle and daub dwelling poached his Lordship's rabbits. Alert gamekeepers meant that 3,000 dead poachers a week and 15,000 dependent widows and children became a drain on the community and the law was changed. Everything became much more humane and a poacher caught in a man trap, instead of having his head blown off, only received a well deserved thrashing from the head gamekeeper.

Display your defences

All of that is beside the point, because our purpose is to deter the passing crook with the static display of defences he sees as he walks by. If this house is hot on the outside then it must be dynamite on the inside! It is meant to impress or depress him, even on a day when a big event is taking place.

Big day precautions

Once the bride is on her way, lock and alarm the house carefully, or leave behind Uncle Jim who can't stand singing hymns. It is upsetting for a thief if he sees a grumpy old man waving by the doorstep and then slamming it forcibly.

The same applies to baptisms and funerals, with the exception that it could be Uncle Jim flat out in the long black limousine, bless him. If it is Jim then pity the house breaker who encounters Aunt Margaret, a regular user of aftershave.

Whoever it is, just remember that someone should be left behind while an event that has been broadcast to the world is taking place. The alarm system is sufficient to frighten off a burglar and protect the home on its own but the tears, uproar and confusion of a wedding or a funeral and the influx of people, some of them strangers, can lead to oversights or deliberate neglect of the alarm system 'just for today'.

Pets are always victims of big days and they are easily infected by the general family delirium associated with a house full of people with unfamiliar smells. To prevent Blackie becoming hysterical and shredding the rented trousers of the gentlemen ushers or pall bearers, he is locked up outside where he can bark his head off at an intruder and be wasting his bad breath.

Deliveries

Careless talk doesn't always have to be careless and a few words spoken in the safest of situations, without fear of being overheard, can equally cause a disaster. I am talking about your trusted neighbour. If you are expecting a delivery of any kind, large or small, and you are going away or the home is unoccupied for a spell, cancel it.

However desperate you are to see your new indoor ski slope do not tell your friendly neighbour, who is holding both the door and the alarm key, that you are expecting a large object, a wedding anniversary surprise for madam which may well turn up in your absence. This is a monumental mistake. First you have given the nice people next door the alarm code, and while he or she is not stupid, they are only required to do their neighbourly duty once or twice a year and because it's a long time since you last asked them they've written it down.

Bogus deliveries

This means that while he or she is doing their duty carefully supervising the workmen staggering in with the box, their house is now wide open, and if the bogus delivery takes place mid-morning or afternoon there will almost certainly only be one Hawkeye watching the delivery lads.

This is going to be a distraction crime and we are now on line for the perfect twin housebreaking. It's that part of the day when he's at work, the kids are at school and she is on her own. Perfect timing! The burglars can't lose on this one because, while she is in your house watching a pair of sweating delivery men have unbelievable trouble with the box, her home is open for inspection by the other member of the delivery team who has modestly remained concealed in the white van. When he enters the supervisor's house he also will be carrying a box.

The bane of boxes

Boxes are the key to everyone's home and carrying one could get you into and out of Colditz in no time. In your case, anyone watching will think that he's from the white van down the road. He won't be greedy going through the neighbour's home and will only take items that will not be noted as missing for a while. The box next door is still proving troublesome and you will have guessed by now that there is a small wiry youth inside it and after the guardian has shepherded his mates outside and they have accepted or declined a cup of tea he will scramble out and interrupt the alarm circuit by jamming a door or window so that it does not close completely.

With a sigh of relief the neighbour watches the white van disappear down the road and comes into the house to reset the alarm. She carefully follows the instructions, but to her horror instead of a row of friendly green lights the box makes a buzzing sound and an unexpected red light winks reproachfully at her. Oh dear, they didn't tell me about this so I'd better switch the whole thing off and ask Jim to have a look at it when he comes home from work.

The house is now disarmed and there's a yobbo free to roam around inside. The benefit for him is that the trusted neighbour is now more concerned about next door than her own home and the aforementioned thefts will not be noticed for some time. Crooks have even delivered wardrobes carrying passengers to empty homes and thoughtfully removed the one they were replacing.

So be adamant with the people next door that you do not want them to accept any deliveries on your behalf. You can also warn them that they too are targets for the white van man.

Packing off packages

Say no to unexpected deliveries quickly and make it clear that you will not accept the item. Tell the person who is either patently honest, or trying to fool you, that you are not interested and that even if he does produce ID he should leave at the speed of light or you will call the police. It is vital that you quickly reach a decision that the package is not for you, because while the front door operator holds your attention and detains you with chatter, the back door man could have entered your home, done a quick sweep and left.

It doesn't take long so make your refusal at the front of the house short and sweet. Distraction crime is mean, nasty and often targeted on the old and vulnerable, so if you are young and bright don't let it happen to you.

Some things are sacred

The moral of the phoney deliveries story is that some things in life are sacred and your burglar alarm code is one of them. Keep the numbers close to your chest. Only disclose them to people who need to know, who are your wife/husband and maybe one other.

Children and security

This is very difficult today because of the phenomenon of latchkey children. The pressures of work at the present time mean that many couples are still at work when school finishes and I don't think it is right for a 14 year-old to be weighed down with the responsibility of switching an intruder alarm system on and off. Yes, I want them to be aware of the importance of home security, but if they are in on the secret that means that we have another voice to talk carelessly.

In spite of all that is said about home protection alarms are still incorrectly associated with protecting objects of enormous value, and a boy or girl might boast at school that they have an amazing Star Trek system at home ' ..and as you are my bestest friend I can tell you that it drives my Mum mad but I can work it. All you do is...'

Before you know it your burglar alarm code has become a game that the kids are playing in the school yard, so please make sure that those very important numbers are not exposed to daylight too often. Crime starts early in the era of slapped wrists and cautions and every classroom in every school in the country has a couple of children that you pray to God your little darlings will not adhere to. Naturally they are the ones with whom our kids end up joined at the hip. It's all fun and games, but the young thug talks to his older brother and the secret is out. Goodbye security!

Final thoughts

Thankfully today, unlike the message in 1940, careless talk doesn't costs lives. Occasionally there is violence in burglary, but in the main the impact of burglary is more psychological than physical. Some victims shiver at the remembrance, others smile ruefully, but underneath the fear and embarrassment there is a deep revulsion and anger. Some person crept through your home, took things that marked the passage of your life and sold them on without a thought to their real value.

Worse still, if the cause of the loss was laziness or lack of care on your part, then make sure from this hour and this day that it will not happen again. You will ensure that in future when you are chatting with friends and acquaintances, and the subjects under discussion are private, confidential and potentially risky you will make absolutely certain that the persons to whom you are talking are the only ones in the circuit. It's a hard lesson to learn so let's look at the reminder list of dos and don'ts.

Dos and don'ts

■ Don't disclose holiday information in a crowded place where it can be overheard – hairdressers, supermarkets, the pub, leisure centre, etc.

■ Don't give the taxi firm a precise pick-up address.

■ Do meet your taxi at a landmark or between two houses, anywhere that does not pinpoint your address.

■ Do ensure that the return date and time for the taxi drop-off is left to the last minute.

■ Don't write precise addresses or dates on luggage labels – street, town and post-code are enough.

■ Don't leave messages in milk bottles or under the front door mat.

■ Do talk face to face with the person who is responsible for the cancellation of your milk, post and newspapers.

■ Do pay extra attention when the security routine of your home is disturbed by a celebration and there are strangers in the property – weddings, funerals, barbecues, etc.

■ Do ensure that your neighbour remembers your alarm code and does not write it down.

■ Do cancel all deliveries and tell your neighbour not to accept any that turn up.

■ Do engage your brain before your mouth!

chapter 9
Burglar Alarms and Insurance

In the security business burglar alarms are known as 'grudge purchases', classed roughly in the same category as road tax and haemorrhoid suppositories, as something you sincerely wish that you didn't have to go into the expense of buying and installing. So you don't! Later, after the burglar has called to change a few minds, the reluctant purchasers want not only bells and son et lumière, but door knobs wired to the mains and towers with War of the Worlds death rays.

The grudge purchase has now become as necessary an acquisition as a car or washing machine, and it's a shame that it takes something as unpleasant as an intruder sneaking around Bob and Doris's bedroom to alert them to the need. Let me spare you the fear and anxiety that they experienced by talking you into adding to your home security an alarm system.

Types of alarm

You would not believe just how sophisticated security alarms are today and how they'll be even smarter tomorrow. At this moment and available are voice, retina and fingerprint recognition systems, along with alarms which allow pets, other than elephants, to roam free in the house. You can have wire-free, solar powered security, and all of this is coming to support the standard CCTV and vibration detectors. There are door phones, smart cards, digital video recorders, and you can have integrated microwave and passive infra-red technology (your dinner cooked and a golden tan thrown in!) and all of this is marshalled to keep the thief at bay.

Are you impressed or is that a question forming on your lips: 'yes, it all sounds absolutely fantastic, but how much is it going to cost me?'

Costing

This is the old 'how long is a piece of string' riddle and the answer of course is as long as you want it to be. The same loose logic applies to the type of security net in which you choose to enmesh your home. What is the value of the items needing protection and how big is the area to be secured? I won't place the family in the equation because we'd be talking billions, but if it comes down to making a financial choice keep your loved ones in mind, because there is nothing you possess that is more valuable.

Computing costs is a risky business, thanks to our financial world bouncing up and down, but in 2006 it was fair to quote £400 to £500 as protection for the average semi. A bigger home, not palatial but one you'd love to buy, would cost £500 to £750 while the superb house that you don't have a snowball's chance in hell of owning unless you are already in it can go from £750 to big bucks, especially if you want singing and dancing and police response.

Having the law around in a trice is a great idea if you live in an area with a low rainfall, but not such a good wheeze in a place where occasional showers are forecast. Some local police authorities forbid police cars to chase escaping burglars or joy riders on wet roads, because it is risky and might lead to officers being taken to court for dangerous driving!

Installing your own alarm

You have a decision to make even before you choose the system that suits your home and pocket. That is whether to install the alarm yourself or to call in a professional security firm to do the job.

Some readers will be handy around the house and would be happy setting up their own home protection, but it's not essential to be a DIY genius. The instructions are on the box and there are only two comical but fatal security errors regularly made by amateurs. These are not the fault of the manufacturers, but are the result of the efforts of some pretty dim amateurs.

First, do not install the control panel where it and its pretty row of lights can be seen by a prospector peeping through the letter box. This is the same letter box I advised you to get rid of.

It is the second mistake that is a court martial hanging offence in the burglar alarm business. When you correctly install your system and power it into life by inserting the three-pin plug into a nearby wall socket, kindly remember that a burglar may gently remove same and render the unit useless!

Insurance

I mentioned earlier that as the population becomes older and more vulnerable, so the incidence of burglary increases exponentially. The result of this is an inevitable across the board rise in insurance premiums for everyone. So is there anything we can do to soften the blow? We moan for ever about ferocious hikes in the price of petrol, but apart from all getting together and not buying one particular brand for a week, which is unlikely, there is absolutely nothing we can do to stop ourselves from being screwed. With insurance however there is a way to coax our insurers into treating us more kindly which will leave both parties pleased.

Insurance is another grudge purchase, fuelled by the legendary company which demands its premiums on the dot, but becomes shy and withdrawn when it comes to paying out on a claim unless we stamp our feet and scream. There may be a grain of truth in this urban myth, but let's face it, if there are plenty of burglars about there must be legions of people dreaming up fraudulent claims. Nothing dramatic or over the top, but you can't really blame the insurer who takes a long, hard look at the latest 'accident at home' claimant pictured in the local rag holding the snooker club champion's cup above his fractured skull with two broken arms.

Taking security seriously

Burglary by day and night in a drug culture is on a scary, upward trend and our insurers will soon be asking for not just our money, but real, concrete evidence that you are taking domestic security seriously. It hasn't quite got to the death and flame thrower stage yet, but if crime continues on its steady climb I can see government introduced security standards on the horizon. Everyone will be compelled to install burglar alarms, British Standard locks, smoke detectors, the lot, and if you think I am becoming a little over excited, here's something to make you change your mind.

For example...

By June 2007 the sale or purchase of property, your home and mine, will include legislation on its efficiency rating. This doesn't mean hanging the washing out in order of precedence, her knickers before his socks, but how the house uses its energy resources. Is the boiler ultra-efficient, is heat lost through the cat flap, does a wooden floor lose points?

For some reason known only to bureaucrats, the efficiency rating is calibrated not from 1–7, but A–G. Arsenal C Liverpool D doesn't sound terribly exciting, but that's how they've decided to do it and I think that after a while, though we are told otherwise, the efficiency rating of a house will affect its value. Triple glazing and solar powered water heating systems good, coal fire and wood burning bad.

Compulsory security

There is a commendable side to the legislation, in that we should be made aware of the clean and full value of uses of energy and this move mirrors exactly my attitude to security. Compulsory security grading will definitely come and when the security inspector outnumbers his energy inspector rival, it will be nice to welcome him with a blast of sound as he attempts to climb in through the upstairs toilet window. If you can't beat them, join them!

Talk to your insurers

Before you decide to either install an alarm yourself or engage a security firm to do the job, consult your insurance company. Some insurers insist that they will only offer reduced premiums if the alarm system and other security aids installed are those they nominate, while others are satisfied if the work is performed competently by an amateur or professional and is up to the British Standards.

This is the moment to weigh up the cost involved and wonder why your insurer is so keen on pushing a particular model onto you. Is it for your benefit or theirs? If the answer is yours go ahead, but there are dozens of brokers out there bursting their jockey shorts to help you find a better deal on your terms. Use them, or complain to your insurer that you are not happy, and that you want an improved offer and might consider moving elsewhere in the insurance community if one is not forthcoming. A deal can always be struck.

chapter 10
Holidays

Naturist holidays have a lot going for them! You have the minimum amount of baggage to carry or be lost by the airline and if a fellow nudist attempts to steal your wallet as you laze around the pool or play volleyball he won't know where to look. If he does manage to lift the thing his next major problem will be where to hide it!

I am told that dispensing with your clothing is an even better way of enjoying a holiday than wearing a postage stamp bikini or posing pouch, but of course the less you take with you, the more you leave at home in an empty house, which can be a bit worrying. Meanwhile the suitcases pile up, and three hours of airport delays later the same bags eventually clank into view on the carousel just as you were giving up hope.

Protecting your valuables

We made it in one piece and here we are on the Costa Lotsa ready to forget real life and just float around until we're the wrong shade of pink. We've worked hard and waited for this break, so no way is anything going to stop us having a good time. And of course we'll be careful with our valuables, we're not stupid.

Holidays don't always work out the way we hope they will, but this one has got off to a great start! You've met a nice couple, had drinks together and the two sets of kids are getting on like a house on fire. There I go again – house, home, I must stop thinking about it and relax. Four more rum and cokes please! I am over the moon that you are having a wonderful time, but don't be too laid back. It's fabulous to leave all the financial and work hassle at home for a few days, but remember – you are not a hippie!

It's OK for those who live in a guitar case to be spaced out, because they really don't have much that is worth stealing apart from a headband, but you, man, are a walking bank and can be spotted a mile off. There may be anonymous tourists, but the average Brit rarely falls into that category, so just go through the whole holiday picture as you doze on the beach. We'll assess your chances of getting through the next couple of weeks and embarking on the return flight having lost nothing but a few layers of skin.

Your luggage

Let's look at the suitcases. You didn't remember what I said, did you? What am I going to do with someone who writes their full address on the label, along with the date and flight number of the return journey? The street, road, avenue, close, building are all more than enough along with the village, town, city and UK postcode. And don't worry if you and the bags fly off on different holidays. As long as the World Centre for Orphan Baggage has that information they will come back like Lassie!

Your handwriting on the luggage labels is very neat and so far the address has been seen by taxi drivers, the mob around the check-in and those people like you enjoying a beer or coffee as you wait to be called to departures or sit out the delay. The baggage loaders have also admired it and the wag who christened London's main airport 'Thiefrow' wasn't just referring to massive robberies.

Advertising your holiday

So I make it about 200 people who have given your bags the once over! You and your family, being decent people, smiled at many of them and you would have done the same to the others if you had known of their existence, but it is not difficult to calculate the mighty host who could, if they wanted to, profit from your very successful advertising campaign. Your address, outward and return dates and destination hotel are public knowledge and you're not even in the air yet!

Looking back at the news it seems that UK airports are easy targets for huge bullion robberies, but if you stay alert and guard the hand luggage you have an excellent chance of arriving at your destination with what you started out with.

Airport security

I'm assuming that your SunSpot holiday is a package, just a no-frills get you there and back deal. Nothing wrong with that and, thanks to the new danger of world terrorism, it may be more secure than travelling on a long haul scheduled flight. You can blame the boarding card stub!

The boarding card stub

This is the little piece of card bearing your name and seat number that you find in a pocket six months later. It brings back a little rush of memories and then you bin it. Some years ago if you were a big time international traveller you could apply to the airline for a Frequent Flier rating. This entitled you to certain privileges and to gain them an applicant had to spill out a lot of personal information which the United States government kept on file. They said that the scheme was a safety measure to keep tabs on terrorists, and as you know by now that I am hooked on the weaknesses and strengths of defence it appeared to be a good idea, but the scheme fell down because of an oversight.

What if a traveller didn't forget the stub, like you and I, but threw it away and I was behind him and picked it up? Being of a naturally inquisitive nature I would log onto the web site of the airline concerned and using the name of the stub chucker do a little digging. It has actually been done, and important personal and confidential information was gleaned about the passenger, his life style and commitments.

I make the point to emphasise that hi-tech is amazing, but nowhere near 100 per cent reliable, and in the end it is the electricity in the human mind that shorts the same power in a machine. The American scheme is no longer in use. From what I hear and see your PIN number may follow the stub into oblivion, as crooks and governments worm their way electronically into our lives and privacy is under attack from all directions. The obvious conclusion is that if you don't defend yours, nobody will.

Protecting your valuables

Your flight has been called, so check that your bags are still there and go. I am not aware of airport departure lounge robbery other than in the duty free shops, so let's set off on the two-mile hike to gate 93. Here again, although it is a safe area and immensely boring, don't relax vigilance. As we thunder along with our trolleys it gives us time to recap.

Your money

For a start you are carrying much more money than you usually stuff into that old leather wallet Uncle Ron gave you a couple of Christmases ago. It looks like it is ready to give birth to ten little wallets and your habit of ramming it into your back pocket, careless at the best of times, is now suicidal, so start thinking of a safe place to put it.

I was told years ago that the best way to carry a cigar and keep it unbroken was to place it inside your sock just below the ankle. The same applies to a wad of money. You can actually purchase a specially manufactured sock-wallet and a surf on the net will lead you to what is on offer. Yellow is apparently the popular choice, which reminds me of a friend who grew tired of losing a sock every time his were washed. He decided to wear only one colour of sock for the rest of his life so that there were always spares. His choice was also yellow, dicey with a dinner suit and at funerals, but it is a piece of logic which appeals to me.

The sock-wallet

If you can apply the same brand of thinking to security you are safe. The sock-wallet has an added bonus in that you can stroll along happy in the knowledge that a potential pickpocket now has to bend at the knee and surreptitiously slide his hand inside your trouser leg to make contact. If you derive any pleasure from this then you'll be dragging him along the promenade for half a mile.

This can be avoided by wearing shorts which of course makes any sock-level robbery out of the question. A large percentage of Brits wear socks with sandals, a mode considered by Armani to be ever so slightly unfashionable, but if it helps security and you want your money to be safe and where you can see it, give it a try!

In the end whatever colour socks and type of trousers you are wearing, discovering a thief about his work will offer you a golden opportunity to give him the toe of your boot. Joking apart, sock-wallets are a very good idea, but wherever you keep you money, etc be sure it is zipped, buttoned or secured safely and regularly check that it is still there.

Travellers' cheques vs bank rolls

Another factor in safely carrying money is that a lot of boodle can be squeezed into one small travellers' cheque. I know that they need countersigning, but they are safe and unlike stolen money, if you lose one you can stop it being used the moment the theft is discovered.

When you pick them up they must be signed and at this stage it is vitally important that you keep the receipt. This records the number of each cheque, is proof of ownership and starts the mechanism to forestall an imposter presenting them.

Another feature is that they come in little books and are less conspicuous than a roll of notes bigger than a turnip, which brings me to a very bad American habit that the Brits have picked up. The bank roll. This is rolling money up in a bundle that would choke a rhino, and I'll discuss the failing when we reach that little bar we'll adopt as our own on holiday. Until then, when you are in public don't put your money on exhibition.

In-flight security

I think you would be mighty unlucky to have anything stolen on the flight. That is no reason to relax normal vigilance and if the cabin crew are taking the trouble to remind you of the airline safety procedures you should do yourself the courtesy of going through your own checklist. Items carelessly left on seats are an invitation, but the majority of flight losses are a result of the frantic scramble to abandon the aircraft the moment it stops rolling.

For some reason many passengers become demented when the seat belt sign goes off and it's 'Out of my way, damn you!' as the coats, bags, laptops and cameras that were so carefully stowed in the overhead locker back home are now pulled out like bad teeth. The result of this frenzy is that smaller objects are pushed to the back of the locker, and as these storage spaces are specially built to be unreachable and unobserved by anyone shorter than Michael Jordan standing on tip toes they are unseen and forgotten.

Well, not completely forgotten. After a couple of minutes on the bus to the arrivals terminal, Mum will suddenly say 'where's the camera?' Too late, because when an aircraft sits on the ground doing nothing it is costing the holiday company big bucks so the cleaning crew is encouraged to work fast. The world record for pouring aboard and collecting every tiny detail of recent occupation – sick bags, sweet wrappers, money, bottles, cans, tissues, cameras, newspapers and binoculars, etc – and ensuring that none of the evidence is seen again is about four minutes. It is said in the airports of the world that if aircraft had those big yellow escape slides that worked upwards the job could be done even more quickly.

Check hand baggage

Forget any valuables left on the aircraft. You might, if you are extremely lucky, find that some generous soul living on a pretty limited income has handed in the artificial leg you left behind, but as I continue to remind you, relying on luck is a risky way to be secure.

Unless the aircraft is full of smoke, do not rush to leave it. Carefully remove your hand baggage, check that you have all small items like cameras and children and make your way in a leisurely fashion to the bus or into the arrivals. There is absolutely no point whatsoever in reaching the carousel 20 minutes before your bags show up unless you enjoy that funny clanking noise as it trundles around. It's also a safe bet that if you are first there with your wonky-wheel trolley your bags will be last off. Don't rush, you are almost on holiday.

Immigration

The next stop is at immigration, which means that you are nearly free to enjoy yourselves. This applies almost everywhere except America. Everyone in the universe is trying to get into the USA, and you have to be patient and not worry that by the time the formalities have been completed you may only have ten minutes of your holiday left.

There is a serious point. A long flight and a big delay when you get there leave you tired, fed up and vulnerable, but enough gloom because at last even with that awful photo in your passport they've let you into their country. You are safely through with your baggage and head for the holiday representative or the car hire desk.

Car hire

Apart from terrorists and turbulence Rent-a-Wreck is the supreme danger point so far. Many holidaymakers are happy to be rid of cars and driving for a couple of weeks, and are content to taxi or be bussed around and I'm on their side. It's purely a personal thing and I understand the more inquisitive who don't like timetables, and the person who always keeps the bus waiting or tells the driver where he's going wrong.

The man I'm watching likes the open road and he doesn't mind driving on the right so he leans on the counter, slightly anxious as he produces various documents and signs forms. He is looking straight ahead, his attention fixed entirely on the girl. How much will the car and insurance be, or if the booking was made several weeks ago is he uttering silent prayers that it has come through or is it lost in cyberspace? He is also wondering what kind of rattler they are going to give him.

The last things on his mind are the items dangling like fruit from his shoulder. It is a harvest of bags, cameras and other stealables and this is how he can either keep or lose them.

Grab and run

One thief will be waiting outside, close by on a scooter. He will be wearing a white shirt and blue jeans so that if you spot him and give a description you will have narrowed the suspects down to about 30 million young men. If he's not on the scooter he will be standing in the doorway, ready to open it and flee when his mate also in uniform snatches a bag and legs it. It happens very quickly so you have no chance. There's a vicious tug on your shoulder, you spin in surprise and your bag is gone.

It is understandable, after a long or even short flight, that a feeling of relaxation and tiredness compounded by the heat and relief on a safe arrival dulls the traveller's sense of awareness. Before you completely keel over as you wait for your bags to show, make a point of deciding which of you will do the car hiring while the other rides shotgun on the trolley. The lucky winner stays with the bags, watching and standing over them like the Monarch of the Glen while the mug sweats his way through renting a car in a foreign country.

Staying alert

The rental process is not all that difficult, it's not even irritating and the staff are always helpful and patient – except those awful people in San Ferriane two years ago… The point that I am making is that however pleasant and efficient the girls are it does take time and this window of opportunity is what the thief is looking through.

Our hero slumps over the counter waiting for the man who got there before him to be fixed up and in the lull his mind strays to a cool drink. Why is it taking so long? He shifts the camera shoulder strap to a more comfortable position and settles in deeper to the counter. How touching it was that he gave his camera a final stroke, because if it and anything else is dangling from his person on a strap, or not firmly anchored between his feet he will shortly be waving goodbye to the lot!

Likewise, he should clutch his credit card, money and documents as tightly as he did as a kid when he ran to the shop with his pocket money for ice cream. His passport should also be carefully guarded and he must be wary of anyone standing just that little bit too close, because if he isn't the holiday is over and he's only been in the country 25 minutes.

Warning stories

Can you imagine the irritation involved in reporting the loss of a passport and waiting for cover if the nearest consular official is three towns away? Tie that up with a bunch of credit cards, money, driving licence, tickets and pills, etc all gone for ever while you sit in a police station when you should be on the beach.

If you had chained an iron ball to each bag it would have been less trouble than going through that nightmare, so when you arrive at your next holiday destination, remember the scenario I have described. The pull on your arm, the cry and a youth seen in the corner of your eye if at all, as he dashes off. What a start to arriving at your dream destination, although not quite as bad as frequently happened at the turn of the previous century to immigrants arriving in New York.

Some, almost penniless, had travelled from as far as Russia and Poland and once they were clear of Ellis Island with their new names they would stand bewildered holding a piece of paper with an address on it. A kindly person would approach a family group surrounded by their battered suitcases and offer to help. He would look at the paper and nod, indicating that he knew the street and that it was close by. General relief all round and after offering to carry a suitcase he would gesture for the family to follow him.

You can guess the rest. The generous soul was a fleet-footed youth and unless Ivan was an Olympian that would be the last he would see of a bag he'd carried several thousand miles. Even if he was quick on his feet the shock was stunning, and the prospect of leaving a pregnant wife and five children alone on a quayside put pursuit out of the question so the thief got away with it.

That is a true picture of how a thief works, and his lack of any feeling for his victim, so next time you travel remember poor Ivan's story.

Vigilance pays

Obviously if it happened to you there would be similar shock and upset, but certainly not the same crushing despair felt by the immigrants. The world is kinder if even more dangerous today, and help and assistance would be on call, but I mention the incident because Ivan's excuse was complete ignorance. What would yours be?

Whatever it is – clumsiness, neglect, or over-confidence – the antidote is to never allow strange and exotic surrounds to throw you off guard. Enjoy the new sounds and smells, and if the language is different remember that the majority of thieves are silent and if your defences are down you won't hear them coming so be vigilant. If you are muttering 'be aware' and 'vigilance pays' in your sleep it will drive your partner bananas, but you won't be burgled. Incidentally did you know that the word 'banana' comes from the Arabic banan, which means finger, so let's raise two banans to the thief and suggest he try somewhere else!

Handbags and hand luggage

The puzzle about handbags and hand baggage is what came first – fashion or the weight restriction on carry-on items? Women's handbags used to be much smaller, with most of their survival kit in the suitcase, but now that the budget airlines have become stricter regarding baggage allowance and volume they pack it all in the bag that is somehow rammed into the overhead locker.

This piece of hand luggage is the larger sister of the handbag, which a thief would prefer to steal. He will assume that Dad is carrying the passports, etc and if he missed that lot at the car hire or in the hanging-around-waiting-aimlessly hall then why not have a go at her larger bag. This will contain jewellery, mobile phone and the camera, which I have already told you not to carry over your shoulder. It would be crazy to remove a valuable object from a dangerous location and place it in a safe one which you do not carefully protect, but people do just that.

To lose items or have them stolen at any time is bad enough, but for a woman to suddenly find herself in a holiday paradise full of beautiful people all looking like Victoria Beckham in formaldehyde is an appalling prospect when she has no make-up, at least for the first few days. This once again proves my old point that items do not have to be worth a fortune to make their loss felt.

Reporting theft

On top of this psychological blow, when the theft is reported the victim can look forward to spending their time sitting inside a police station, with last night's walking wounded, instead of enjoying themselves on the beach. I could also have said 'if' the theft is reported because there is another type of victim, who determined not to have the holiday ruined, writes the whole business off and ploughs on.

Always report theft. The first question your insurance company will ask is 'did you report the incident?' If your answer is 'no, it wasn't worth bothering about and you know what the French/Italian/Spanish/Mongolian police are like!' then you can't complain if your insurers reply 'yeah, we know what they're like and we can't be bothered to pay out so thank you for calling. Goodbye!'

The hassle involved in cancelling credit cards, travellers cheques – you did remember to keep the receipt with the cheque numbers in a separate place – arranging new tickets and finding the nearest British consular official to ask for advice on what to do about a stolen passport is pretty daunting. And all around you people are having a great time, sometimes sparing a sympathetic smile and walking off whispering 'those are the poor people who were robbed.'

Arriving

I'm painting a pretty black scenario, but that is what it will be like and you can avoid the nightmare simply by being on the ball and guarding what is yours. Don't allow some spotty youth with bad teeth to wreck your holiday by picking on you as a stupid, wealthy tourist. All tourists are assumed to be wealthy and stupid, so be smart and take advantage of his blazing sun without paying for it twice. Hold on to your belongings and watch them

carefully, however hot and tired you feel. Politely decline unso-
licited offers of help unless you are absolutely convinced that the
98 year-old threatening to guide you around the ruins is slower
on the hoof than you are!

It is vital to remember that after the excitement of the big day,
the packing and the flight, it is the actual arrival which leaves
you at your most vulnerable. All you want to do is get to the
hotel, check in, find your room and take off your shoes. Next it's
a shower, a clean shirt and a stiffener at the bar to complete the
transplantation. It won't take long to have you back on track so
make sure that you and your bags have reached the rum and
coke stage together.

Not like the older couple you spoke to in arrivals, who said that
they were staying at your hotel but didn't get on the coach or
appear at reception. Hope they didn't have anything stolen.

The balcony soars over a sea so blue that at the horizon it melts
into the sky. There is a gentle breeze stirring the palm trees and
carrying the perfume of jacaranda on the warm air. The beach is
of pure white sand and crowded with people reclining under
brightly coloured umbrellas. Some are playing games or swimming in the pure clear water, while local thieves add to the
atmosphere of relaxed wellbeing with demonstrations of traditional crafts such as removing unattended objects. Away from
the promenade in the nearby mediaeval quarter throngs of
smiling tourists thread their way through the narrow streets
fending off eager waiters and stall owners. They pay little attention to the activities of early twenty-first century pickpockets
practising their trade.

I glued that together from several holiday brochures and slipped
in a bit of my own. Obviously the brochures can't go overboard

on the danger in the streets and on the beach, but I can because this book isn't about selling flights and hotel rooms. It's about home and personal security and the unpleasant fact that like rats a thief is never very far way.

I also honestly want things to be seen in the proper perspective with no exaggeration or emphasis in the wrong place, so ask yourself this. Have you ever been robbed on holiday? No. Do you know of anyone who has been robbed on holiday? I'll bet the answer is in the affirmative, which means that so far you have been either aware of your security responsibilities or very lucky and they weren't as wise or fortunate. The danger is always there and thieves wouldn't be in business if they were slow to react to the way we submit to the numbing effect of foreign places.

The hotel

Back in the hotel we've unpacked, showered off the dust of travel and changed. The kids have already disappeared with strict instructions to be back at zero hour, so we'll take stock of the room again. The first glance takes in the jumble of smaller items emptied from pockets and handbags and now scattered over any flat surface. The hotel has our passports so we can forget about them, but the financial and nuisance value of the rest of the items is considerable.

Protection and threats

The room itself has two doors which are the main entrance from the corridor and the balcony door. Most people are always careful to lock the room door, but often leave the balcony open because it's on the fourth floor and who is going to risk his life climbing that high? He won't have to if he can swing across from next door's balcony! With a bit of luck an agile thief need only gain entry to one room to do the whole floor, so lock your balcony door when you leave the room.

If your room has windows check that they lock securely and take into account the fact that if the accommodation is not structurally part of the hotel you may have a problem. If it is called the Hotel Bombolini complex, and you are in a chalet or structure close to the hotel and it is robbed, in some cases the management will not accept responsibility. It might be worth checking on this when you arrive.

The safe

You've finished your room examination and are left with an ugly thing standing in the corner. I will ignore any cheap cracks, because this is important. I am talking about the room safe! You hire it, read the instructions and save yourself a host of problems. It is simple to operate and we choose our own code to open and close it. Maybe it looks out of place and unattractive, but it wouldn't be a good idea to try to lift and carry it into the bathroom. The safe is what it says it is! 'I will keep your valuables secure, but it is only fair to point out that I have one major defect. To hire me will cost you a couple of euros per day.'

That's... let me work it out over two weeks. Why that's over 40 euros down the pan! In a fortnight at the end of the holiday, after nobody tried to mug us, pick our pockets or burgle the room when we were on that boring excursion to the glass factory, what have we got to show for it? What a waste of money!

Negative response to security

In the world of burglar alarms, barking dogs and all other forms of security they call this the NRS. Negative response to security. It is based on the assumption that if looking back no threat manifested itself, then it didn't exist! This attitude is completely bananas because the holidaymaker is looking at the situation in a mirror. It's the wrong way round. What they should say at the end of a wonderful two weeks or more untouched by sneak thieves and Montezuma's revenge is 'we had a knock-out holiday' and nothing else. They wouldn't show us their boring holiday film with Dad saying '...and this is us not being robbed in the cathedral.'

Money well spent

So stop any problems before they start. All of this is logical and obvious, but it is very hard to convince people that some of their holiday money can be usefully spent on other things besides ice cream and sangria. You can soften the pain by remembering that the outlay is nothing compared to what a thief has taken from you, so please use your room safe. It is more accessible than the big one behind reception in the manager's office, but if you feel happier leaving the family diamonds there go ahead. All I ask is that objects of value are left in a secure place, which is going to cost you less than a couple of rounds of drinks or toasted sand-wiches on the beach.

How to stay safe

We have to carry money and credit cards on our person at all times, but the difference between doing it in a temperature of 25° Centigrade on holiday and battling through life and work at home is that we will be wearing considerably less and lighter clothing! This is alarming, because if a robber can lift your wallet when you are wearing a heavy winter coat how much easier it must be for him when he can actually see the lump that isn't part of the body!

Most robbers recommend that you stuff your money in your sun hat or back pocket, so I think you'll have a better chance of hanging on to it if it's in an inside pocket of your shorts, or safe in the aforemen-tioned sock-wallet. If you can see it and feel it then it's still there.

Day and night vigilance

Half of your holiday will be spent in the dark which traditionally is the rush hour for robbers. This is not strictly true, for although they need to wear sunglasses, many are perfectly happy to pick your pocket or bag-snatch as the sun shines. In daylight, if you have been dipped, at least there's a chance that you may spot him, whereas at night the shadows are on his side and he's gone. On the other hand, if you are the victim of a gang it doesn't really matter what time of day or night the theft took place because your wallet, etc will have passed through several pairs of hands before you know that it has gone.

The real blow is that even if you recognise the culprit he'll be happy for you to search him, because he hasn't got it and you will be very embarrassed and angry. Save that red face by, how many times do I have to say this, carrying only what you need and keeping it in a safe place.

Keeping money safe

We've already discussed the ankle wallet and there's a refinement on this if you don't mind walking around feeling like a private eye. This is the holster wallet. People usually wear money belts around the waist, but this one fits around the chest and over one shoulder with the pouch under arm. It means you have to wear a shirt, but it will save you money on sun cream, protect the treasury and perhaps thieves will think you are a cop.

That roll of notes

You've budgeted for each day and, while it is inevitable that there will be a 'must have' in the leather shop, you've got a pretty good idea of how much cash you should be carrying backed up by a credit card, right? This is where the bad habit I mentioned earlier comes in. It is the practice of rolling money in bundles instead of folding it flat. It may impress your new lady friend when you pull out your roll, but there's a chance that there will be others even more impressed and they aren't thinking about kissing you.

To me a big roll of notes denotes brash carelessness. It says 'I've got plenty. I could lose this and not even notice!' A chubby bunch of fingers full of gold rings will reinforce that attitude and believe me, in five minutes every thief in the neighbourhood will be on call.

It is always better to keep money clipped and folded flat and even if you are on holiday in the Republic of Urangsir where the exchange rate is a joke, never go out carrying more than 50 million palonkas. That also applies more seriously to countries where you end up carrying the local currency in thousands instead of the tens, 20s and sometimes 50s that we are used to and it can become a little overwhelming.

The drunken haze

The local hooch can have the same effect, and if you are turned over in a drunken haze then you are a mug and thoroughly deserve it. Bars and pubs are there to be enjoyed, and most thieves like a beverage or two, so watch the passing scene with both eyes and keep the other one on your wallet.

Ending the holiday safely

The holiday is drawing to its close. The hotel food was okay, the kids had a magic time and thanks to the sun you are now on your fifth nose. You used the room safe and lost nothing, the portables like handbags, cameras, wallets and mobile phones still belong to you and the money just lasted out. You remembered that you don't want too many people to know your return date and phoned home to remind your trusted neighbour to make that last minute pick-up call to the taxi company.

From her we learned that the alarm hadn't gone off and that not much had changed in the lifetime that you had been away. She had milk, bread, eggs, etc for you and was confident that she would receive the postcard of the hotel, which you sent on the first day, in the next three months.

Looking back I am absolutely delighted with your full marks on advanced security and was impressed when you didn't just give your credit card to the waiter in that restaurant, but took it to the cashier and watched the process taking place. Identity fraud is widespread and horrific examples of accounts being slaughtered come up every day, but you were aware of that.

It takes time to pick up and adapt to new routines and longer still to drop bad ones, but you have done very well on this holiday... up to now! Sadly I have to tell you that there is still time to come unstuck and it would be a tragedy if you fell at the last fence!

Going home

As Britons we believe that most foreign airports are a mixture of noisy shambles and utter chaos. We see crowds milling round staff who appear to be indifferent to their wishes. There is a host of tongues and no apparent controlling hand and you are on a downer. The rep has abandoned you for the next wave of tourists and, if you hired a car, they've spotted a little dent on the off-side wheel arch which wasn't there when you drove away two weeks ago.

All of this, on top of a ten-mile queue at check-in and no trolley, has sent you back in time to the moment you arrived. Then you were tired and vulnerable, but now you are totally cheesed off and even more open to attack.

There are people who live in airports. Some are fascinated by the through-put of people and the strange mixed atmosphere of excitement, fear and weariness. Others are thieves who keep on the move so as not to attract attention from the security officers, but a good place to spot them is around the television screens which tell the pink faces gazing helplessly upwards that their flight is delayed. Is that our flight? Rampant grumpiness sets in, inflamed by frustration, and it is the thief's last chance to strike before you disappear through the departure doors. Don't lose the game in the last minute.

You are home. The holiday was great with no disasters apart from Dad's hugely embarrassing attempt to join the flamenco dancers on the last night and real life now begins again. Nice to be back, and as you move amongst all of the familiar objects that make your house a home you've no time to think that the alarm has done its job, because there are suitcases to empty and the washing machine to be fed. And it's raining!

Dos and don'ts

- Do wait until the last convenient moment to order your taxi to the station or airport. If the cab driver or his friends are crooks such a brief window of opportunity will force them to pass up the opportunity.

- Don't give the taxi company precise details of your address when ordering a cab. You can give them a landmark or other feature which will enable the driver to find you.

- Do be outside with your bags when the cab arrives as this will further increase doubt of the exact location of your home.

- Don't print your address in detail on luggage labels. Name, street, city, town or village and UK postcode are sufficient to bring them home if they stray.

- Do be vigilant during the wait involved in checking in and the dead period before you go through departures. If there is a delay, frustration and disappointment, particularly amongst children, often diverts adult attention from security.

- Don't place small objects – cameras, binoculars and mobile phones – in the aircraft overhead lockers. In the rush to cram baggage into the locker nearest to your seat these items will be pushed to the rear of the locker and either damaged or forgotten in the even more hurried dash to disembark.

- Do be vigilant at the low points of your holiday – delays, diversions, tired or careless on arrival at your destination – and the same on your return. Remember, thieves are watching and they know how travellers look and feel.

- Don't go to the car hire counter looking like a Christmas tree with cameras, bags and other items dangling from your person. Take only the essential documents and leave the decorations with the person standing guard over the main body of the baggage.

- Do check the windows and doors of your hotel room. Even if your accommodation is on the 99th floor, never leave the room unoccupied with a balcony door open. Thieves move up and down like spiders, but people forget that they also move sideways like crabs.

- Do use the safe in your hotel room. I am going to say this twice! Do use the safe in your room. It costs you some of your holiday money, but it saves you from hair loss and floods of tears if a thief pays a call. As an alternative some folks lodge their valuables in the hotel manager's safe, but as the man says, the choice is yours.

- Don't carry large amounts of money or flash rolls of it in public. Commonsense, but in a happy, generous holiday atmosphere...

- Do take lots of money in travellers' cheques and only carry a daily ration of cash, plus a modest reserve for madam when she spots a 'must have' in Ali's bazaar.

- Don't carry a wallet in the back pocket of your shorts, or money in the band of your sun hat. You are on holiday and wearing fewer clothes than usual, which means that what was concealed in cold weather back home now sticks out like a sore thumb.

- Do conceal your money where you can see and feel it. Inside pockets and sock-wallets are favourites, but you know your body better than I do and I leave final destinations to the owner.

- Do check what is happening to your credit card in restaurants and shops. It is good security to take it to the cashier yourself. Here again, you are no techno wizard, but he doesn't know that. What he has learned is that you are security conscious and if he's straight it will not bother him. If he's a crook you will have spoiled his day. Good.

- Do remember as the holiday comes to a close to call your friendly neighbour back home and remind them to book your taxi under the same conditions that you ordered one on the outward leg – last-minute booking and no precise address. Taxi drivers are going to hate me for this, so I should make it clear that I believe the great majority to be as decent as the rest of the population. Sadly it's the rotten apple theory again, so just be careful.

I've spent a lot of time on this chapter because I feel that you, your family and your home are one entity. You bring some of it with you on holiday and you want to go back with the same, so when a situation mentioned in this chapter arises, think, act and you will win the battle against the thief.

chapter 11
Michael Fraser's Outro

Well, there it is! The low-down on how to gear up your home security by using the old grey matter and without major expense. Looking back and knowing what you know now, I bet you were surprised at some of the giveaways I opened your eyes to. It now all seems so simple and obvious.

When you set up obstacles you deprive the thief of his most valuable commodity, time. Remember, though, your deterrents must be visible – clean, serviced alarm boxes, Neighbourhood Watch stickers, closed gates, padlocks, secured wheelie bins, no litter of ladders and tools, and all in all a general air of tidiness and care.

Put yourself in the yob's position, but instead of being a thief he is now a mugger on a quiet street. Coming towards him from one end is a pensioner on a zimmer frame, while from the other direction Arnold Schwarzenegger is approaching. The mugger's choice is obvious, so relate it to your home security: if you choose to be the old gentleman with the dripping nose it means I have failed. Don't let me down because I'd much rather see you as the Terminator!

Muscle up your home

Alternatively, if you decide to follow my advice to muscle up your home it signifies two things. You and your family are safe and I don't have to return to a life of crime! Three things really, because it also indicates that your attitude to security has changed, and you have become aware of so much inside and outside the home which can lead to risk and loss. There are countless times in every 24 hours when we are vulnerable to danger in varying degrees, but throughout the whole spectrum of crime there is one constant factor – time.

Whatever the crook's business, he wants it done as quickly as possible. In the burglar's case he is a coward, a bundle of nerves who just wants to steal your possessions and take off fast. Consequently anything you do to shrink his time-safety window will instantly put him off raping your home. Don't fret about dashing his hopes. He'll wipe away a tear and bravely soldier on to assess the other 40 million dwellings in the UK, safe in the knowledge that 39 million plus will be push-overs.

The safe habit

That's what it all boils down to. You may have become tired of my constantly repeated mantra about deflecting a thief onto someone else's home, and think it callous, but come on… If the man next door doesn't give a damn about security, and won't listen to commonsense as he watches you set up your firewalls, surely he deserves what is most likely to happen. You made the effort to get into the burglar's mind, you changed your habits and routines, and security became part of your life like learning to drive or use a computer. There is no escape from cars and computers today and in a dangerous world the same applies to security. So please digest what I have written and be safe.

In conversation with friends and strangers the subject of this book has in every case resulted later in comments like, 'since you mentioned the catflap... free range wheelie... infra-red post code marking... I've taken steps to...' Once you start thinking and acting as I do you will be safe. I can guarantee it!

Index